JUDICIAL INSTITUTIONS IN NINETEENTH-CENTURY LATIN AMERICA

Judicial Institutions in Nineteenth-Century Latin America

Edited by

Eduardo Zimmermann

Institute of Latin American Studies
31 Tavistock Square, London WC1H 9HA
http://www.sas.ac.uk/ilas/publicat.htm

Nineteenth-Century Latin America Series

The Institute's Nineteenth-Century Latin America series results from the annual workshop on nineteenth-century Latin American history held at the Institute, and is aimed at encouraging the study of various aspects of what has largely been a neglected period in the modern historiography of the region. The General Editor of this series is Eduardo Posada-Carbó, Senior Lecturer in History at the Institute of Latin American Studies.

Publications in the Series

No. 1   *Wars, Parties and Nationalism: Essays on the Politics and Society of Nineteenth-Century Latin America*
Eduardo Posada-Carbó (ed.) – 1995 (out of print).

No. 2   *In Search of a New Order: Essays on the Politics and Society of Nineteenth-Century Latin America*
Eduardo Posada-Carbó (ed.) – 1998

No. 3   *Independence and Revolution in Spanish America: Perspectives and Problems*
Anthony McFarlane and Eduardo Posada-Carbó (eds.) – 1999

No. 4   *Judicial Institutions in Nineteenth-Century Latin America*
Eduardo Zimmerman (ed.) – 1999

No. 5   *The Politics of Religion in an Age of Revival*
Austen Ivereigh (ed.) -- forthcoming

Institute of Latin American Studies
School of Advanced Study
University of London

British Library Cataloguing-in-Publication Data
A catalogue record for this book is available from the British Library

ISBN   1 900039 30 3

Institute of Latin American Studies
University of London, 1999

Contents

Acknowledgements

I would like to thank all the authors, commentators and participants at the Fourth Nineteenth-Century History Workshop: 'The History of Justice in Nineteenth-Century Latin America', organised by the Institute of Latin American Studies, University of London, where all the papers included in this volume were presented. Thanks are also due to Victor Bulmer-Thomas, Director of ILAS at the time of the workshop, and to his successor as Director, James Dunkerley, for their support of the annual workshops, and especially to Eduardo Posada-Carbó for his enthusiasm and his patience.

Eduardo Zimmermann

Notes on Contributors

Linda Arnold is Professor of History at Virginia Tech. She is the author of *Bureaucracy and Bureaucrats in Mexico City, 1742–1835* (1988) and *Política y justicia: La Suprema Corte Mexicana, 1824–1855* (1996). She serves on the editorial boards of *Historia Mexicana, Anuario Mexicano de Historia del Derecho* and *Secuencia.*

Osvaldo Barreneche (PhD University of Arizona) is currently Profesor Adjunto at the Universidad Nacional de La Plata, Argentina. A specialist in the history of criminal justice in Argentina, he was assistant editor of *The Presidio and the Militia of the Northern Frontier of New Spain* (1997).

Charles R. Cutter (PhD University of New Mexico) is Associate Professor of History at Purdue University, where he teaches Latin American and Spanish borderlands history. Elected to membership of the Instituto Internacional de Historia del Derecho Indiano in 1992, Professor Cutter has written on a variety of aspects of Spanish colonial law, including the prize-winning *The Legal Culture of Northern New Spain, 1700–1810* (1995).

Víctor Uribe (PhD University of Pittsburgh) is Assistant Professor of History at Florida International University. He has recently completed a book on the history of lawyers, society and politics in Colombia, 1780–1850. His work has been published in several academic journals.

Thomas Holloway is Professor of Latin American History at Cornell University. He is the author of *Policing Rio de Janeiro: Repression and Resistance in a 19th-Century City* (1993) and a number of other books and articles on the social and institutional history of Brazil. He is currently Vice-President and President Elect of the Latin AmericanStudies Association.

Eduardo Zimmermann (DPhil., University of Oxford) is currently Associate Professor and Director of the Department of Humanities at the Universidad de San Andrés, Argentina. He is the author of *Los liberales reformistas. la cuestión social en la Argentina 1890–1916* (1994) and he has published numerous articles on Argentine history.

Law, Justice and State-Building in Nineteenth-Century Latin America

Eduardo Zimmermann

One of the common themes of this volume of essays in the history of judicial institutions is the interaction between the legal world and the wider political, economic, social and cultural processes through which the transition from colonial status to independent nationhood took place in nineteenth-century Latin America. Rather than looking at this transition as a radical transformation of judicial institutions and practices, many of the studies in this book place particular emphasis on the continuities between these two phases.

The clash between the cultural and institutional legacy of the colonial world and the modernising principles of liberal nation-building is, of course, a recurrent theme in the historiography of the region. Nineteenth-century Latin American elites embraced liberalism as an antidote to what they saw as the backwardness inherent in Spanish institutions and values. The creation of a liberal individualist society meant, among other things, the establishment of legal equality, with the ideal of the rule of law and a commitment to the protection of individual rights, private property and the enforcement of contracts. Thus, it has recently been argued that in nineteenth-century Latin America the struggle to create a viable legal order was one of the ideas 'at the heart of the liberal project after Independence, which ever since have formed a critical part of the mythology of Latin American liberalism'.[1] In addition to the close relationship between the world of law and the internal composition of Latin American political elites (legislators and ministers were overwhelmingly lawyers), this juridical bent of Latin American liberal nation-building was expressed in the enthusiastic efforts made by those elites in favour of constitutionalism, codification and the setting up of new judicial systems at the local and national level. The conviction that a rationally conceived body of written laws and its application by an independent authority would effectively protect individual liberties and organise political power persisted throughout the century, despite the erosion caused by the successive impacts of different strands of historicism and positivism on legal thought. It also persisted despite the

---

[1] Vincent C. Peloso and Barbara A. Tenenbaum (eds.), *Liberals, Politics, and Power. State Formation in Nineteenth-Century Latin America* (Athens, GA and London, 1996), p. 1. Also, Frank Safford, 'Politics, Ideology and Society', in Leslie Bethell (ed.), *Spanish America after Independence, c.1820–c.1870* (Cambridge, 1987), pp. 85–6.

fact that, as a result of recurrent political instability, these formal constitutions and codes at times appeared to be a dead letter.[2]

Clearly, the struggle to establish the rule of law as part of the nation-building project in nineteenth-century Latin America was burdened by the particular circumstances in which that process took place. Among those particular historical circumstances, historians have frequently emphasised the legacy of the colonial world, deeply embedded in a hierarchical, centralist and corporativist ethos.[3] The disappearance of effective state power after Independence, the centrifugal effects of strong regionalist movements alongside economic structural imbalances also helped to consolidate the *caudillista* tradition of strongly personalised power. This frequently led to political instability and the concentration of all functions of administration, legislation and judicial power in one person, making impossible the functional differentiation necessary for the process of rationalising the law.[4]

Far from being an abstraction evoked to explain all the ills and shortcomings of the new independent nations, the corporatist legacy of the colonial world was in fact present in very concrete collective actors, such as the army and the church. This presence was also felt in very concrete social practices, such as church and military *fueros*, the special jurisdictional privileges enjoyed by the clergy and military officers, which reinforced a system of legal, social and economic stratification, and appeared to be wholly incompatible with the ideals of legal equality embraced by liberal nation-building.[5]

Two different sets of questions can be addressed at this point: first, what were the actual judicial practices of the colonial order like, in terms of their fairness and ability to respond to the needs of colonial society, and what effects did they have on the daily life of the majority of the people? And second, what were the consequences of the survival of *fueros* and le-

---

[2] For the political and ideological contexts of constitutionalism and constitution making in nineteenth-century Latin America see Safford, 'Politics, Ideology and Society', and Charles Hale, 'Political and Social Ideas in Latin America, 1870–1930', in Leslie Bethell (ed.), *The Cambridge History of Latin America*, vol. IV (Cambridge, 1986).

[3] Richard M. Morse, 'Toward a Theory of Spanish American Government', *Journal of the History of Ideas*, vol. 15, 1954, pp. 71–93; 'The Heritage of Latin America', in Louis Hartz (ed.), *The Founding of New Societies* (New York, 1964); Glen Dealy, 'Prolegomena on the Spanish American Political Tradition', *Hispanic American Historical Review*, vol. 48, February 1968, pp. 37–58; Howard J. Wiarda, 'Law and Political Development in Latin America: Toward a Framework for Analysis', *American Journal of Comparative Law*, vol. XIX, Fall 1971, pp. 434–63; 'Toward a Framework for the Study of Political Change in the Iberic-Latin Tradition: The Corporative Model', *World Politics*, vol. 25, January 1973, pp. 206–35; Claudio Véliz, *The Centralist Tradition of Latin America* (Princeton, 1980).

[4] On *caudillismo*, see Frank Safford, 'The Problem of Political Order in Early Republican Spanish America', *Journal of Latin American Studies*, vol. 24, Quincentenary Supplement, 1992; John Charles Chasteen, 'Making Sense of Caudillos and 'Revolutions' in Nineteenth-Century Latin America', in John Charles Chasteen and Joseph S. Tulchin (eds.), *Problems in Modern Latin American History. A Reader* (Wilmington, Delaware, 1994); Noemí Goldman and Ricardo Salvatore (comps.), *Caudillismos rioplatenses. Nuevas miradas a un viejo problema* (Buenos Aires, 1998).

[5] Safford, 'Politics, ideology and society', pp. 52–3, 85–6.

gal privileges, particularly military *fueros,* on the judicial practices of the independent period, and, again, how did this reflect on the interaction between the judicial system and the everyday life of the common people?

Charles Cutter's chapter, 'The Legal Culture of Spanish America on the Eve of Independence', touches upon the first set of questions. Against the received wisdom which depicts colonial judicial administration as 'ponderous, tyrannical, arbitrary and corrupt', Cutter's revisionist work offers a new insight into the virtues of a system which proved to be much more in tune with the needs of the peoples of the different regions of the empire than modern historians have been willing to concede. Cutter describes this system as 'a New World version of Spanish law'; 'a legal system anchored in medieval European tradition and modified by New World circumstances', and explains the process of creation of an original 'colonial legal culture'. One of the key elements allowing for this adaptability, says Cutter, was the *arbitrio judicial,* the degree of personal discretion exercised by the colonial magistrate in the judicial process, particularly at the moment of pronouncing sentence. Although nineteenth-century Latin American codification was, to a large extent, inspired by a desire to eliminate the discretionary powers of the judiciary, and many often misinterpreted it as mere capriciousness, the *arbitrio judicial* made the law a flexible, organic entity that the local populations adapted to meet situations peculiar to their regions. This flexibility was particularly suited to 'a corporatist world where unbridled individualism was not a virtue, [and] the ideal of community well-being took precedence over personal gain'. Colonial magistrates, according to Cutter, exercised their *arbitrio judicial* to work towards solutions between contending parties that conformed to 'community expectations of fairness'. Thus, fairness *(equidad)* and local custom tempered the application of the general framework defined by written law and *doctrina,* allowing for distinctive regional variations, and opened up a process of negotiation between various strata of the different communities which created what Cutter defines as 'the consensual hegemony' of Spanish rule.

Linda Arnold's work deals with such other questions as the consequences of the survival of military *fueros* for the judicial practice of early independent Mexico. Brian Loveman has recently suggested that the adoption of military *fueros* in Latin American constitutionalism reflected the infusion of nineteenth-century liberal nation-building with military authoritarianism:

> Much of Latin America experienced unremitting rebellion and civil war in the nineteenth century. Appeal to extraordinary powers became a habit ... In practice, liberalism and authoritarianism merged ... Military force made authoritarian liberalism possible. The privileges and immunities (fueros) carried over from the colonial era often exempted military officers from civilian courts ... here too, constitutions played an important role. The constitutions of independent Spanish America charged the military with protecting the political system, conserving internal order, defending the government against internal subversion [and maintaining law and order]. In effect, the military

became a fourth branch of government, with constitutionally defined status and a political mission. With some exceptions, the military retained the colonial fueros and expanded tremendously their political role. Almost any coup, any barracks revolt, or any local uprising could be justified as an effort to preserve the constitution or restore constitutional government purportedly threatened by government abuses. Latin American constitutions invited, indeed demanded, military participation in politics.[6]

Setting aside the political consequences of military *fueros* for independent Mexico, Linda Arnold carries out an extensive analysis of military, constitutional and ordinary jurisdiction case files and shows that 'judges applied jurisprudence not corporate biases when they decided guilt or innocence, determined liability, and issued definitive sentences'. In her conclusion, Arnold states: 'There is no evidence to suggest that justice was any more or any less privileged in the military corporation than in ordinary jurisdiction'. Moreover, the persistence of the *fuero* is not explained as a symptom of the power of a culturally determined corporate structure, but as the result of innumerable individual actions: 'The *fuero militar* did not persist in Mexico simply because eighteenth-century reformers initiated it, and some elite political leaders believed in preserving a tradition. No, the *fuero militar* persisted because thousands of people — plaintiffs, outlaws, abandoned wives and abandoned children, privates and corporals, attorneys and judges, guards and officers — actively asserted agency, albeit some not voluntarily, in corporate society. And some of those active participants in corporate society believed they would lose advantage were they cast adrift in the amorphous and violent public culture that the military tried so hard yet failed to contain throughout the early national era'.

In my view, both Cutter and Arnold offer a fertile reevaluation of corporate institutions as channels of assertion for common people in societies largely shaped in a non-individualist mould. The conflict between liberal discourse and traditional society is also taken up, although from a different perspective, by Thomas Holloway and Osvaldo Barreneche, in two chapters dealing with the role of judicial systems in the process of state-building in nineteenth-century Brazil and Argentina, respectively. In the first of these chapters, Holloway argues that the contradictions of a liberal ideology within a highly stratified society help to explain the failure of the experiment in locally elected justices of the peace and its eventual replacement with appointed representatives of central authority, in the Brazilian judicial reform of 1841. Thus, an appropriate innovation in the top-down judicial system established since the colonial age, says Holloway, succumbed to the socio-political realities of the era.

---

[6] Brian Loveman, *The Constitution of Tyranny. Regimes of Exception in Spanish America* (Pittsburgh, 1993), p. 6.

In Osvaldo Barreneche's chapter, the continuities between the colonial and national periods are very clearly perceived, given that, as the author argues, in early nineteenth-century Argentina, 'institutional experimentation and adaptation of colonial state forms occurred simultaneously'. Political instability and a lack of material resources characterised the administration of criminal justice in Buenos Aires, where the public careers of judicial officials were often tied to the fate of the political faction (federalist or unitarian) in power. Through a careful description of the procedures followed by *jueces de paz*, criminal judges, and police *comisarios*, Barreneche paints a picture of excessive police intervention in this process which gave the government the means to intervene and control judicial and crime-related issues. In his conclusions, Barreneche elaborates on a theme first developed by José Carlos Chiaramonte: post-colonial judicial order in Buenos Aires featured certain non desirable aspects — i.e., autonomous police practices and a dilatory administration of justice — that were originally conceived as being provisional.[7] However, in the long run these traits became permanent features of the system. Judges frequently had to accept the increasing power of other law enforcement agents, such as the police, and the use of arbitrary power by these agents became 'a characteristic feature of the modern penal system in Argentina'. As in Holloway's work, the contradiction between liberal discourse and everyday practices is central to Barreneche's evaluation:

> Politicians, lawmakers, and jurists recognised the significance of liberal principles as basic components of the post-independent penal system in Argentina. However, they concluded that the application of criminal justice based on this creed was not possible because of unstable political circumstances. Thus, debates regarding the ideal role of the judiciary and criminal law conceptualised the new penal system as a result but not as an instrument in the consolidation of new state forms. Meanwhile, the adaptation of colonial criminal procedures applied by empowered law enforcement agents not only functioned as a transitional figure in the post-colonial judicial structure but also remained as a permanent feature of the system.

The scarcity of human resources for an adequate institutional organisation and the overlapping of politics and the judicial system are themes that are also present in the chapters by Víctor Uribe and myself. Uribe studies the debate that took place all over Spanish America concerning the abundance of colonial lawyers, a debate which ironically would be followed by laments over scarcity of lawyers during the early republican period. Again, the emphasis is on the relationship between these debates and the state-building and political processes.

---

[7] José Carlos Chiaramonte, 'El federalismo argentino en la primera mitad del siglo XIX', in Marcello Carmagnani (coord.), *Federalismos latinoamericanos: México/Brasil/Argentina* (Mexico, 1993), pp. 81–3.

The question of the actual numbers of lawyers in colonial Spanish America is analysed by Uribe using a very fruitful comparative approach. Within the region, the River Plate concentrated the highest number of lawyers relative to population (although, in absolute terms, Mexico led the field, followed by Peru and Nueva Granada). Nevertheless, as Uribe reminds us, those numbers pale, and the consequent impression of an overabundance of lawyers in colonial Spanish America is dramatically altered, when compared to the number of attorneys found in late eighteenth and early nineteenth-century France, England, or the United States.

If objectively it was not the number of lawyers that created this unease, the political climate of the late colonial era certainly contributed to the perception of *abogados revoltosos* as problematic. The participation of lawyers in 'revolutionary' activities, and more generally in the creation of 'an embryonic public sphere' were among the reasons which encouraged stricter control of the growth of the profession and its regulation. I have found similar arguments in my research on the education of lawyers in Argentina´s Organización Nacional, particularly exemplified in Juan Bautista Alberdi's attacks on the proliferation of lawyers and men of letters in general as detrimental to political order and economic growth. 'El único producto nacional y propio de las universidades de Sudamérica es el doctor en leyes o abogado', lamented Alberdi.[8]

Spanish repression of lawyers' revolutionary activities resulted in the depletion of the profession's ranks during the Independence period, says Uribe, and ultimately led to a relative scarcity in the national period, which explains the development of judicial systems administered by lay citizens during a good part of the nineteenth century. Eventually, Mexico, Argentina and Colombia had to face a serious problem in their quest for the professionalisation and institutionalisation of the new judicial systems: the limited supply of qualified lawyers and the consequent shortage of personnel was a serious hindrance to the successful development of the new institutions. The new republics had to accept that an improvement in the training of lawyers and jurists and the expansion of legal studies in the universities was badly needed in order to fill the new positions in the magistracy and public administration in general. In doing so, Uribe suggests, Spanish American liberals 'ended up expanding even further the liberal (provincial, upwardly mobile) ranks and generally deepening liberal reforms'.

In my own chapter on the education of lawyers and judges in Argentina's Organización Nacional I have also dealt with the issue of the relative abundance or scarcity of lawyers as perceived in the mid-nineteenth century public debate, connecting it with the larger polemics on the different types of education needed by the new nations. Despite the persistent complaints

---

[8] Juan Bautista Alberdi, *Escritos Económicos (1876)*, in *Escritos Póstumos* (Buenos Aires, 1895–1901), vol. I, chapter 8.

in the press and official reports regarding the lack of well trained lawyers to fill the positions created by the new judicial systems, traditional education in the humanities was seen by many as the main culprit for an alleged overabundance of lawyers and men of letters in general, and the negative consequences arising from their activities, culminating in growing demands for the expansion of technical instruction and an education in the sciences.

I have also analysed the ways in which the contents of the courses taught at Argentine universities, particularly in civil and constitutional law, reflected the changing views of jurists, politicians, and statesmen concerning the institutional models to be followed, whether the matter at hand was the regulation of marriage, inheritance or the relations between national and provincial governments.

As can be seen from the variety of viewpoints presented in this collection, the inextricable link between law and politics was a central feature of the state building process in nineteenth-century Latin America. The contrast between liberal ideals and authoritarian practices; the rationalisation of the law and the political manipulation of judicial processes; the elites' dreams of modernisation and institutional innovation and the realities of traditional societies rooted in the colonial past: all these polarities indicate that ultimately the dynamic interplay between continuity and change that characterised nineteenth-century Latin American societies was particularly salient in the evolution of judicial institutions, and was certainly not going to disappear in the transit to the present.

CHAPTER 1

The Legal Culture of Spanish America on the Eve of Independence*

Charles R. Cutter

The centrepiece of Spain's colonial regime was a legal system anchored in medieval European tradition and modified by New World circumstances that provided the basis for the political and social ordering of the Indies. Here was a government of judges, an administrative apparatus where nearly every appointed official exercised some sort of judicial authority. And although the Bourbon monarchs assumed a more interventionist role than had the Habsburgs in colonial administration, especially in matters economic, many in the eighteenth-century Hispanic world held dear the traditional notion that, above all else, the prime function of the crown was to dispense justice.[1] The legitimacy ascribed to the legal system as mediator of conflict was fundamental to the colonial order, and subjects of the crown defined themselves and found identity largely in juridical terms — through special jurisdictions, privileges and restrictions. The legal system served as a constant venue of negotiation between the various groups and individuals who comprised this hierarchical society. Over the course of several centuries of Spanish rule, there developed in the Indies a legal culture, Castilian in spirit but distinctively American in form, which reached even the remotest parts of empire.

Creating a legal culture in the Indies

In any of the major cities of Spanish America, of course, an intellectual community of jurists gave erudite polish to this colonial legal culture. Thanks to the early establishment of universities, colleges and other insti-

---

* This essay draws substantially from portions of my book, *The Legal Culture of Northern New Spain, 1700–1810* (Albuquerque, 1995).

[1] This notion of the proper role of monarchy persisted well into the late-Bourbon period. In 1785, for example, Lorenzo Guardiola y Sáenz wrote that 'the true occupation of the king is to do justice in his kingdom'. Lorenzo Guardiola y Sáenz, *El corregidor perfecto y juez exactamente dotado de las calidades necesarias y convenientes para el buen gobierno económico y político de los pueblos* (Madrid, 1785), pp. 38–9, quote on p. 35. An early articulation of this notion is found in *Las siete partidas del Sabio Rey don Alonso el Nono* (Salamanca, 1555; facsimile reprint, Madrid: Boletín Oficial del Estado, 1974), 2.1.1. See also Colin M. MacLachlan, *Spain's Empire in the New World: The Role of Ideas in Institutional and Social Change* (Berkeley, 1988), pp. 8–13; Benjamín González Alonso, *El corregidor castellano (1348–1808)* (Madrid, 1970), p. 18.

tutions of higher learning, young men from well-placed *criollo* families gained access to the tightly controlled world of the juridical elite. In this atmosphere, colonials drank in the intellectual and philosophical traditions that underlay Hispanic law, they acquired the skills necessary to become members of the judicial elite and they imparted this esoteric knowledge to subsequent generations of *criollo* jurists. By the seventeenth century, juridically trained native sons occupied important positions as ministers in *audiencias* and as *catedráticos* in universities.[2] The existence of a cadre of well instructed *criollo* jurists was an important dimension of the colonial legal culture, for it helped legitimise, and give resonance to, a New World version of Spanish law. Imbued with the guiding principles of the Castilian and *ius commune* traditions, *criollos* brought those intellectual systems to bear on circumstances they faced as Americans.

Just as important as an elite community of jurists in the creation of a colonial legal culture was the very approach employed by Spain in the administration of its empire, for it was largely juridical in nature. The primacy of law as an instrument of political and social control was evident from the earliest moments of Spain's New World endeavour. Indeed, the establishment in 1508 of the Audiencia of Santo Domingo set the tone for a juridical cast to royal administration in the Indies. Years ago, C.H. Haring aptly characterised the *audiencia* as 'the most important ... institution in the government of the Spanish Indies' precisely because it stood 'at the centre, the core, of the administrative system'.[3] As the colonial state developed, New World *audiencias* played a much more conspicuous role and wielded considerably more power than their peninsular counterparts, the *chancillerías*. The pronounced juridical character of New World administration is readily apparent at this upper echelon of government.

Spanish administration, however, relied not only on well-trained jurists who served as *oidores* in the *audiencias*, but also — and perhaps to an even greater extent — on a host of other officials to whom the crown entrusted with the care and wellbeing of the monarchy. From the powerful viceroy to the local *juez de aguas*, a network of multicompetent personnel existed that ensured the presence of the crown throughout the Indies. Although most lacked formal legal training, these men invariably wielded the crown's *vara de justicia*, and they administered their respective jurisdictions largely through legal mechanisms. As magistrates in court, of

---

[2] On the elite legal culture, see Javier Barrientos Grandón, *La cultura jurídica en la Nueva España* (Mexico City, 1993), which focuses primarily on the literary underpinnings. On *criollos* as *audiencia* ministers, see Mark A. Burkholder and D.S. Chandler, *From Impotence to Authority: The Spanish Crown and the American Audiencias, 1687–1808* (Columbia and London, 1977); as teachers, Clara Inés Ramírez González and Armando Pavón Romero, 'De estudiantes a catedráticos. Un aspecto de la Real Universidad de México en el Siglo XVI', in *Claustros y estudiantes: Congreso Internacional de Historia de las Universidades Americanas y Españolas en la Edad Moderna* (Valencia, 1989), pp. 279–89.

[3] C.H. Haring, *The Spanish Empire in America* (New York, 1947), p. 126.

course, they prosecuted criminal activity, resolved conflict among dissatisfied parties and maintained social order. In attending to other responsibilities, too, they utilised juridical forms and models. Indeed, documents that we today might consider to be essentially administrative reports typically assumed the format of a legal proceeding — one need only think of the classic administrative instruments of the colonial period, the *auto* or the *dictamen*. In sum, the essence, the very form of Spanish colonial administration helped create a colonial legal culture — that is, certain shared values, general knowledge and expectations about the law — that touched all strata of society in all parts of the Indies.

In this piece, I wish to focus on this more generalised and quotidian level of the colonial legal culture. How did ordinary colonial subjects understand and approach the law that held sway in the Indies, the legal corpus known as *derecho indiano*? How did *derecho indiano* function on a daily basis? By examining the construction and spirit of *derecho indiano*, we can appreciate how this fluid and malleable legal system met both the needs of the crown and the expectations of local subjects.

The construction of *derecho indiano*

In its fullest sense, *derecho indiano* encompassed all law that applied to the New World, and it stemmed from a variety of sources. These can be categorised into two major groupings — one of peninsular provenance, the other of New World origin. In the first group was legislation that rested upon the Castilian normative system as established in the *Ordenamiento de Alcalá* (1348) and reaffirmed in the *Leyes de Toro* (1505), *Nueva Recopilación de Castilla* (1567) and *Novísima Recopilación de Castilla* (1805). This juridical ordering gave preeminence to royal legislation, and it had general application throughout the realm. Beneath royal laws came the local *fueros*, or municipal charters, to which judges were to resort if no specific royal law applied. On the third tier, applicable only in the absence of royal law or municipal *fuero*, stood the *Siete Partidas*, a thirteenth-century text attributed to Alfonso X of Castile that sustained the juridical notions of Roman and canon law. It was through this legitimisation of the *Partidas* that certain aspects of European *ius commune* — especially procedural elements — became fixed in Castilian law.[4]

Because the Indies were the patrimony of the crown of Castile, the Castilian normative system served as the general model for the New World and, initially, *all* Castilian law had automatic force in the Indies. A major turning point in the creation of a discrete body of *derecho indiano* occurred in 1614, however, when, in recognition of New World distinctiveness, Philip III determined that only laws formulated specifically for the

---

[4] Francisco Tomás y Valiente, *Manual de historia del derecho español*, 4th ed. (Madrid, 1983), pp. 243–7. On the controversy surrounding the authorship and date of the *Partidas*, see pp. 237–42.

Indies would have force there.[5] The appearance of the *Recopilación de Indias* (1680) signalled the consolidation of a particular legal ordering for the colonies, emblematic of a distinct American identity.

In contrast to laws that emanated from the peninsula were those of New World origin, what some have termed '*derecho indiano criollo*'.[6] Royal officials and institutions — viceroys, *audiencias*, governors, *corregidores* and *alcaldes mayores* — issued much of this legislation, but settlers also had a hand in shaping this ultramarine dimension of *derecho indiano*. Especially prominent was the activity of municipal *cabildos* in regulating local urban affairs. Indigenous law, too, carried weight in a supplemental capacity, as long as it did not conflict with royal legislation or European notions of religion.[7] As the colonial period unfolded, and as subjects and royal administrators established a legal order to fit their world, the numbers of laws specific to the Indies grew impressively. By the eighteenth century, *derecho indiano* had acquired a character quite distinct to that of Castilian law. While these two sets of written law — Castilian and local in origin — served as the foundation for *derecho indiano*, there was much more to *derecho indiano* than mere legislation.

Despite its fundamental role in shaping and defining society, Spanish colonial law has remained something of a mystery to modern scholars. Perhaps because of the great chronological and ideological distance between ourselves and the *antiguo régimen*, modern historians have often joined with nineteenth-century patriots and foreign observers in denouncing the colonial legal system. Judicial administration is still often depicted as ponderous, tyrannical, arbitrary and corrupt.[8] More careful scrutiny of the historical record reveals an intricate legal system that proved to be adaptable to the peculiar needs of the diverse regions of empire. Local modification of Hispanic law — *derecho vulgar* — was an important feature of this flexibility and constituted a legitimate expression of local self-governance.

---

[5] Tomás y Valiente, *Manual*, pp. 339–40.

[6] For example, see Abelardo Levaggi, *Manual de historia del derecho argentino* (Buenos Aires, 1991), t. 1, pp. 144–6; Alfonso García Gallo, *Metodología de la historia del derecho indiano* (Santiago, 1972), p. 60.

[7] Tomás y Valiente, *Manual*, p. 341.

[8] Benjamin Keen, *A History of Latin America* (Boston, 1992), pp. 101–2; Charles Gibson, *Spain in America* (New York, 1966), p. 109; Stanley J. Stein and Barbara H. Stein, *The Colonial Heritage of Latin America* (New York, 1970), p. 81. Some examples of nineteenth-century comments are found in Levaggi, *Manual de historia del derecho argentino*, vol. 1, p. 203; Michael C. Meyer and William L. Sherman, *The Course of Mexican History* (New York and Oxford, 1991), p. 314. Commenting on New Mexico, Josiah Gregg, *Commerce of the Prairies* (Norman, 1954), pp. 164–5, asserted that 'there is scarcely one *alcalde* in a dozen who knows what a law is'. An almost identical assessment was offered by W. W. H. Davis, *El Gringo: New Mexico and Her People* (New York, 1857; reprint, Lincoln, 1982), pp. 105–6, who stated that 'none of [the *alcaldes*] were ever accused of knowing any thing about law', and that 'the decision of the *alcalde* was seldom made up according to the merits of the case'. See also David J. Langum, *Law and Community on the Mexican California Frontier: Anglo-American Expatriates and the Clash of Legal Traditions, 1821–1846* (Norman, 1987), especially pp. 131–52.

No doubt the misguided view of Spanish colonial law — and the consequent failure to recognise *derecho vulgar* — stems not only from cultural distance, but also, for English-speakers, from language problems. In truth, there exists no exact English equivalent for the Castilian word '*derecho*', though the word 'justice' might come close.[9] Roman law, which greatly influenced Spanish law of the early modern period, made a clear distinction between *ius* — that which is just — and *lex* — a duly promulgated norm, usually written. So, too, did the various Iberian legal systems (though the vernacular *derecho* came to replace *ius*).[10] Heirs to Castilian institutions, jurists in the New World approached the task of making and interpreting law in much the same way as their peninsular counterparts.[11] The *letrado* community certainly distinguished between '*ley*' and '*derecho*'. So, too, did the general population. One rarely argued that the '*ley*' was on his or her side; instead a litigant approached the court seeking one's justice, or '*su derecho*'.[12] Jurists and community alike conceived of Spanish colonial law in this wider sense. People expected their proper '*derecho*', and magistrates endeavoured 'to give to each his own'.

In general terms colonial magistrates were to exercise their experience, knowledge and prudence in meting out justice.[13] More specifically, they drew from a system that sought justice somewhere in the convergence of written law, *doctrina* (the opinions of jurists), custom and *equidad* (a communally-defined sense of fairness).[14] Under the rubric of written law one must include not only true *leyes reales* (technically only the Castilian cortes could initiate these), but also other written statutes that had the ef-

---

[9] In *A New Pronouncing Dictionary of the Spanish and English Languages* (New York and London, 1900), Velázquez defines 'derecho' as 'right, justice, law, equity'.

[10] See Alfonso García Gallo, *Manual de historia del derecho español*, 9th ed. (Madrid, 1982), vol. 1, pp. 161–4 and vol. 2, pp. 40–8.

[11] Though laws formulated specifically for the Indies always took precedence over Castilian law, the Crown usually sought compatibility between the two systems. See, for example, *Recopilación de Indias* 2.2.13; in a similar vein, 2.1.2. For a closer scrutiny of this issue see Bernardino Bravo Lira, 'El derecho indiano y sus raíces europeas: derecho común y propio de Castilla', *Anuario de historia del derecho español*, vol. 58 (1988), especially pp. 5–35; Tomás y Valiente, *Manual*, pp. 337–41.

[12] Quote in Spanish Archives of New Mexico (SANM) II:160, María Martín v. Luis López, 30 April–30 May 1710.

[13] The idea of balance in approaching the art of jurisprudence appears as early as the *Partidas* and extends well into the nineteenth century. *Partidas*, 3.3.3, for example, states that judges must be 'de buena fama. E sin mala cobdicia. E que ayan sabiduria, para judgar los pleytos, derechamente, por su saber, o por vso de luengo tienpo. E que sean mansos. E de buena palabra, a los que vinieren, ante ellos, a juyzio, E sobre todo, que teman a Dios'.

[14] *Equidad* should not be confused with the more narrowly defined 'equity' of Anglo legal tradition. Particularly important works in identifying the components of *derecho indiano* are Víctor Tau Anzoátegui, 'La noción de ley en América Hispana durante los siglos XVI a XVIII', *Anuario de filosofía jurídica y social*, vol. 6 (1986), pp. 193–232; and Abelardo Levaggi, 'El concepto del derecho según los fiscales de la Segunda Audiencia de Buenos Aires (1784–1810)', in *Actas del VIII Congreso del Instituto Internacional de Historia del Derecho Indiano* (Santiago: *Revista Chilena de la Historia del Derecho*, 1987), pp. 245–59.

fective force of royal law — *pragmáticas, mandamientos de gobierno, provisiones, cédulas, órdenes, cartas, sobrecartas* and so forth.[15] *Doctrina* encompassed the written opinions of both national and international jurists who commented not only on Roman and canon law, but also on royal law.[16] Local usage and long-standing practice also carried the weight of authority under the Hispanic system. This respect for local particularism, even when *contra legem*, has been perhaps the most overlooked dimension of the Spanish colonial legal system.[17] Finally, judicial decisions were to be equitable solutions that not only satisfied the aggrieved party, but also considered the wellbeing and harmony of the community. In a stratified eighteenth-century colonial society, ideas about equity might well differ from ours. Yet a clearly identifiable ray of distributive justice served as a guiding light for colonial magistrates to 'give to each his own'.[18] Keeping these various elements of *derecho* in mind, magistrates were to consider the merits of each distinct case and make a decision accordingly.[19]

Because of this casuistic approach, the precise formula for meting out justice might change, if ever so slightly, with every case. The colonial magistrate, whether a learned *oidor* or a local *alcalde*, exercised a great deal of personal discretion in the judicial process, especially in pronouncing sentence. Known as *arbitrio judicial*, or judicial will, this feature of the system figures as the key to the flexibility of Spanish colonial legal administration. The ambiguity of ju-

---

[15] For a fuller treatment of the range and types of 'laws', see Alfonso García Gallo, 'La ley como fuente del derecho en Indias en el siglo XVI', in *Estudios de historia del derecho indiano* (Madrid, 1972), pp. 169–285.

[16] See Víctor Tau Anzoátegui, 'La doctrina de los autores como fuente del derecho castellano-indiano', *Revista de Historia del Derecho*, vol. 17 (1989), pp. 351–408.

[17] Important work has been done in this respect by Víctor Tau Anzoátegui, 'La costumbre como fuente del derecho indiano en los siglos XVI y XVII: estudio a través de los cabildos del Río de la Plata, Cuyo y Tucumán', in *III Congreso del Instituto Internacional de Historia del Derecho Indiano* (Madrid, 1970), pp. 115–92. For the American south-west under Spanish rule, Malcolm Ebright argues strongly for the importance of custom in Hispanic law. See, for example, his 'Introduction: Spanish and Mexican Land Grants and the Law', in Malcolm Ebright (ed.), *Spanish and Mexican Land Grants and the Law* (Manhattan, Kansas, 1989), pp. 3–11; Malcolm Ebright, 'New Mexican Land Grants: The Legal Background', in Charles L. Briggs and John R. Van Ness (eds.), *Land, Water, and Culture: New Perspectives on Hispanic Land Grants* (Albuquerque, 1987), pp. 15–64.

[18] The notion that the prime goal of justice was 'dar a cada uno lo suyo' appears, even on the northern frontier of New Spain, repeatedly throughout the Hispanic world of the *antiguo régimen*. SANM II:316, Martín Hurtado v. Jacinto Sánchez, 23 April–26 April 1722. *Partidas* 3.1.3, 'E los mandamientos de la Iustitia, e del derecho son tres. El primero, que ome biua honestamente, quanto en si. El segundo, que non faga mal, nin daño a otro. El tercero, que de su derecho a cada vno'. José Juan y Colón, *Instrucción jurídica de escribanos, abogados, y jueces ordinarios de juzgados inferiores* (Madrid, 1795), p. 1, 'La justicia es una constante y perpetua voluntad de dar a cada uno lo que es suyo'. José María Alvarez, *Instituciones de derecho real de Castilla y de Indias* (New York., 1827; facsimile reprint, Mexico City, 1982), p. 21, 'La justicia, tomada en general, podemos decir que es: la observancia de todas las leyes que previenen no dañar a otro, dar a cada uno lo que es suyo y vivir honestamente'.

[19] See Levaggi, 'El concepto del derecho según los fiscales', pp. 245–59.

dicial authority perhaps bothers modern jurists and scholars more than their colonial counterparts, who understood the purpose of *arbitrio judicial.*

Largely misinterpreted as mere whimsy or capriciousness, *arbitrio judicial* allowed Spanish law to be much more than the mechanical application of judicial prescriptions (the trend in Latin American and Spanish law during the nineteenth century was towards codification that sought in large measure to eliminate the discretionary powers of the judiciary).[20] Through this device, law became a living, organic entity that the local population — citizens and administrators alike — might mould to meet situations peculiar to the region. This mechanism, as well as others, empowered Spanish subjects to modify legislation that they deemed to be unreasonable, unjust or harmful to the community.[21] Locals often played a significant role in shaping the legal culture of a particular region.

Derecho indiano in action

Given the range of possibilities, upon which of the various strands of *derecho indiano* did colonial magistrates rely? Certainly, the *oidor* who sat on one of the thirteen late-colonial *audiencias* had a much richer repertoire — textually and intellectually — than did a magistrate at the local level. Highly trained professionals invoked the authority of all pertinent sources of *derecho indiano* — law, *doctrina*, custom and *equidad* — and drew from the sources that seemed to best fit a particular case.[22] It should be noted that we can never be sure of the exact judicial reasoning in the verdict, because the Castilian and, by extension, colonial legal systems forbade magistrates from

---

[20] See Bravo Lira, 'El derecho indiano y sus raíces europeas', pp. 67–79; on the codification process in Spain, Tomás y Valiente, *Manual,* pp. 465–557.

[21] *Recopilación de Indias* 2.1.24 states that all royal provisions must be obeyed, 'salvo siendo el negocio de calidad, que de su cumplimiento se seguiria escandalo conocido, ó daño irreparable, que en tal caso permitimos, que haviendo lugar de derecho, suplicacion, é interponiendo por quien, y como deba, puedan sobreseer en el cumplimiento'. See also *Recopilación de Indias* 2.1.22; *Nueva recopilación* 4.14.2; *Novísima recopilación* 3.4.4; *Partidas* 3.18.29–31. On other mechanisms for altering legislation, see Víctor Tau Anzoátegui, 'La ley "Se obedece pero no se cumple". En torno a la suplicación de las leyes en el derecho indiano', *Anuario Histórico Jurídico Ecuatoriano,* vol. 6 (1980), pp. 55–110. On the idea that laws must be reasonable, Levaggi, 'El concepto del derecho'. Various texts that affirm this right can be found in García Gallo, *Manual de historia del derecho español,* vol. 2, pp. 105–6.

[22] In this respect, a most valuable collection of arguments of a prosecuting attorney (*fiscal*) for the Audiencia de Buenos Aires in the late-eighteenth century is Abelardo Levaggi, *El virreinato rioplatense en la vistas fiscales de José Márquez de la Plata,* 3 vol. (Buenos Aires, 1988). See also Levaggi, 'El concepto del derecho'. Other valuable sources include the Colección Mata Linares housed at the Real Academia de Historia, Madrid, and the writings of a colonial Mexican jurist, Juan de Torquemada, found in the Biblioteca Nacional (Madrid), ms. 20311, 'Varias alegaciones jurídicas que el Lic.do D. Juan Antonio de Torquemada, Abogado de la R.l Avdien.cia de esta Nueva España, dixo en sus reales estrados, en los de su Real Sala de el Crimen, y en los de el jusgado, y avdiencia ecclesiastica', 1724–5.

issuing a written explanation (*sentencia fundada*) of their decision.[23] From all evidence, however, these learned judges remained faithful to traditional modes of procedure and maintained their prerogative of *arbitrio judicial* even in the climate of enlightened despotism and increasing regal control in the late eighteenth and early nineteenth centuries.[24] In a sense they refused to become mere judicial bureaucrats who applied the written law and insisted, instead, on remaining true judges who dispensed justice.

While magistrates in the busy centres of empire had a full arsenal of textual and institutional resources at their disposal, those on the peripheries did not. Economies that could not support centres of learning, great libraries and multitudes of judicial functionaries simply did without. In fact, *most* provinces of New Spain and other viceroyalties made do without a fully staffed judiciary.[25] Honed to the essentials, judicial administration in these extensive marginal areas nevertheless squared unmistakably with the Spanish legal tradition. And in these peripheral zones we can perhaps better appreciate the tremendous strength and flexibility of the Hispanic legal culture. In the following discussion, the primary focus is on New Mexico and Texas, two provinces in the far north of New Spain, but my subsequent research on judicial administration in other regions within the jurisdiction of the Audiencia de Guadalajara seems to confirm a generalised approach to legal affairs.

Streamlined and simplified, nearly all phases of the judicial process in northern New Spain lay in the hands of local magistrates, the most important of whom was the provincial governor. For the most part, frontier governors were proven military figures — a prime attribute in a region on chronic military alert. Able and educated they may have been, but no evidence suggests that the governors of New Mexico or Texas had any formal instruction in law; nor, in contrast to other areas, did they enjoy ready access to a legal adviser (*asesor letrado*).[26] Other local magistrates (*alcaldes mayores* or *alcaldes ordinarios*), drawn from the civilian population, had even less.

---

[23] María Paz Alonso Romero, *El proceso penal en Castilla (siglos XIII–XVIII)* (Salamanca, 1982), p. 260; José Sánchez-Arcilla Bernal, *Las ordenanzas de las audiencias de Indias (1511–1821)* (Madrid, 1992), p. 315, Ordenanzas de Palafox, 'Ordenanzas para la Rl. Audiencia desta Nueua España, Ministros y officiales della', tít. 1, n. 24. On the problems that this prohibition poses, see Francisco Tomás y Valiente, *El derecho penal de la monarquía absoluta (siglos XVI–XVII–XVIII)* (Madrid, 1969), p. 182. Still, we can gain a fairly good idea of judicial reasoning by examining the arguments of the *fiscales* (state prosecutors) of the *audiencia*. Steeped in a common intellectual tradition, these officials no doubt shared with the *oidores* the underlying juridical assumptions that might decide a particular case.

[24] Besides the above mentioned works by Abelardo Levaggi, see Tau Anzoátegui, 'La costumbre como fuente del derecho indiano', pp. 115–92; Tau Anzoátegui, 'La noción de ley en América Hispana', 193–232; especially Tau Anzoátegui, 'La doctrina de los autores', pp. 351–408. See also Levaggi, 'El derecho romano en la formación de los abogados argentinos del ochocientos', *Derecho*, vol. 40 (1986), pp. 17–33; Bravo Lira, 'El derecho indiano y sus raíces europeas', pp. 5–80.

[25] This is explored more fully in Charles R. Cutter, 'La magistratura local en el norte de la Nueva España: El caso de Nuevo México', *Anuario Mexicano de Historia del Derecho*, vol. 4 (1992), pp. 29–39.

[26] Joseph McKnight, 'Law Books on the Hispanic Frontier', *Journal of the West*, vol. 27 (July 1988), p. 75. Ricardo Zorraquín Becú, *Organización judicial argentina en el período*

Not surprisingly, magistrates in northern New Spain — and, for that matter, in many other parts of the empire — approached legal administration with less sophistication than their learned urban counterparts.[27] The scholarly erudition and elegant Latin employed by practitioners of the *mos italicus* surely were lost on many a frontier magistrate. Thus, *doctrina* usually played a lesser role in local judicial affairs, but it was not entirely absent.

While some have argued or insinuated that local magistrates were oblivious to the fundamental legal texts, a closer examination reveals the error of these assertions.[28] There were many such texts in circulation in northern New Spain that can be classified as legal commentary or *doctrina* (though admittedly written in Castilian, rather than Latin and, hence, targeted at a less refined judiciary). Habsburg-era titles such as *Política indiana* by Juan Solórzano Pereira, *Curia philippica* by Juan de Hevia Bolaños, *Instrucción política y práctica judicial* by Alonso de Villadiego, standard fare in any colonial judicial library, also found their way to northern New Spain. So, too, did the works of later, more practical-minded jurists, who shied away from using Latin and who focused more on royal law than on Roman and canon law.[29] One such work, *Instrucción jurídica de escribanos, abogados, y jueces ordinarios de juzgados inferiores* by José Juan y Colón, turned up in both New Mexico and Texas in the late eighteenth and early nineteenth centuries.[30] While admittedly sparse, documentary evidence demonstrates the existence and use of these texts in northern New Spain. More striking still, litigants on occasion invoked the

---

hispánico (Buenos Aires, 1981), pp. 82–3. Although the prominence of the *asesor letrado* rose in the eighteenth century, some *gobernaciones* had such a figure at an earlier date. See *Recopilación de Indias* 5.2.37, 5.2.39.

[27] Even in the peninsula, magistrates at the local level had little formal training in law. For contemporary commentary on this state of affairs, see José Berní y Catalá, *Instrucción de alcaldes ordinarios, que comprehende las obligaciones de estos, y del amotacén* (Valencia, 1757), p. 1; Vicente Vizcaíno Pérez, *Tratado de la jurisdicción ordinaria para la dirección y guía de los alcaldes de los pueblos de España* 4th ed. (Madrid, 1802; reprint, Madrid, 1979), pp. 33–4.

[28] In addition to allusions noted in footnote no. 9, see Marc Simmons, *Spanish Government in New Mexico* (Albuquerque, 1968), p. 176; and more recently, Langum, *Law and Community on the Mexican California Frontier*, p. 33, who cites Simmons.

[29] McKnight, 'Law Books on the Hispanic Frontier', pp. 75–8. For an extended essay on colonial juridical bibliography, see Javier Malagón Barceló, *La literatura jurídica española del Siglo de Oro en la Nueva España* (Mexico City, 1959). Useful discussions of the evolution in styles of Hispanic juridical writing are found in Bravo Lira, 'El derecho indiano y sus raíces europeas', pp. 36–77, and in Tomás y Valiente, *El derecho penal*, pp. 85–151.

[30] Juan y Colón, *Instrucción jurídica de escribanos*. McKnight, 'Law Books', p. 78, finds a 1787 edition of this work in San Antonio, Texas; for New Mexico, SANMI:252 Settlement of estate of Manuel Delgado, 'Inventario', 29 September 1815, lists this as 'Colón de escrivanos'. Governor Joaquín del Real Alencaster made a rather cryptic allusion to the 'formulario de Colón', Archivo de la Real Audiencia de Guadalajara, Biblioteca del Estado de Jalisco (ARAG), Criminal 45–13–1023, Joaquín del Real Alencaster to Señores de la Real Audiencia [de Guadalajara]. Santa Fé, 1 July 1805. This may well be a reference not to the work of José Juan y Colón, however, but to the manual composed by Félix Colón de Larriátegui, *Juzgados militares de España y sus Indias* (Madrid, 1797).

authority of the *doctores* in their arguments.[31] Contrary to the conventional view of universal judicial ignorance, some frontier magistrates did, indeed, consider *doctrina* in their judgements.

Written law, however, figured more prominently than doctrine in the construction of *derecho indiano*. Nearly every territorial jurisdiction of the Spanish empire had at its disposal the fundamental compilations of laws and ordinances — the *Recopilación de Indias, Nueva Recopilación de Castilla, Novísima Recopilación, Ordenanzas de Intendentes* and so forth. Northern New Spain was no exception.[32] Contemporary court proceedings include frequent allusions to 'these laws of the Indies', to 'the royal laws' or, less frequently, to a specific piece of legislation.[33] This evidence suggests not only that magistrates (and litigants) were aware of these basic juridical texts, but also that they consulted them. In addition, one must keep in mind the never-ending stream of *cédulas*, orders and decrees sent to all jurisdictions of New Spain. Since public proclamation of new legislation was one of his functions, the alcalde certainly would be well informed on many affairs, including judicial matters. Similarly, local magistrates were familiar with the various *bandos de buen gobierno*, issued periodically by either the *cabildo* or the provincial governor. The accessibility and authority of written law ensured that colonial magistrates considered it when making their judicial decisions. Assertions that these officials were unaware of written laws are ill-founded.

While *doctrina* and written law constituted important bases for legal practice in colonial Spanish America, custom and *equidad* loom as perhaps the most

---

[31] An example of some rather sophisticated notions of what constituted *derecho* appear in SANMI:464, Petition of Diego Torres, Bartolomé Truxillo, Antonio de Salazar, Manuel Valerio, and Manuel Martín, n.d. (but probably early to mid-eighteenth century). These men argued that their position was supported by 'Ley, authoridad, doctrina, e opinion, assi en el [derecho] civil comun, o canonico'. They also cited Juan Solórzano Pereira's *De indiarum iure* by book, chapter, and number.

[32] Rothrock List, 'Books in Colonial New Mexico', ms. in University of New Mexico General Library, Special Collections. McKnight, 'Law Books on the Hispanic Frontier', *passim*. See also, Eleanor B. Adams and France V. Scholes, 'Books in New Mexico, 1598–1680', *New Mexico Historical Review*, vol. 17 (July 1942), pp. 226–70; and by the same authors, 'Two Colonial New Mexico Libraries, 1704, 1706', *New Mexico Historical Review*, vol. 19 (April 1944), pp. 135–67. Basic texts such as these seem to have been readily available in all parts of the Spanish colonies. See, for example, Jorge Luján Muñoz, 'Acerca de la llegada y aplicación de la recopilación de las leyes de Indias en el Reino de Guatemala, 1681–99', in *Memoria del simposio hispanoamericano sobre las leyes de Indias* (San José, Costa Rica, 1984).

[33] For example, SANM II:508, 'Año de 1749. Demanda puesta p.r Manuel Sanz de Garuizu, En nom.re de d.n Antonio de tapia vez.o de la Ziudad de Mex.co de la Cantt.d que en ella se expresa, Conttra Jph Romo de Vera vez.o de estta villa'. 3 November 1749–14 July 1751; SANM II:360, 'Caussa Criminal Contra Ant.o Yuba yndio natural del Pu.o de tezuque y Asensio Povio Yndio natural del Pueblo de Nambé de la naz.n teguas'. 25 June–2 August 1731; Archivo General de la Nación (México) (AGNM) Provincias Internas 32, exp. 10, 'Año de 1730. Caussa Criminal hecha p.r muertte de Nicolas Pasqual conttra Philipe de Abila actor y reo en el'. 12 April–18 May 1731. An allusion to Article 283 of the Constitution of 1812 in SANM I:216, Ursula Chaves v. Joaquín Pino, 1821.

critical elements of *derecho indiano* and surely served as the well-spring of *derecho vulgar*. As noted earlier, custom was the vehicle by which local entities throughout the empire might modify or reshape generalised judicial practice. And although the conventional view is that of an absolutist imperial Spain, the crown never imposed complete control. Indeed, a surprising degree of self-government existed at local levels during the *antiguo régimen*.

Custom — that is, reasonable and just activity that over time acquires legal sanction — found expression in various ways. One obvious and important form of judicial custom resulted from time-honoured local practice or usage.[34] Throughout the Indies, legal experts — some of whom fell into the regalist camp — consistently recognised the legitimacy of custom as a source for colonial law.[35] Not only the elites, however, but also the lesser lights of colonial society had a hand in establishing and defining customary practice. While imperial administrators and the 'better sorts' of colonists may have been guardians of the dominant culture, the constant negotiation between various strata created, even in the formal setting of the law, what might be termed the consensual hegemony of Spanish rule.[36] For example, like indigenous subjects throughout the empire, the *pueblo* indians learned to play the legal game in admirable fashion. Their continual activity in the courtroom led to the incorporation of certain customary rights into the legal culture of the province. The so-called '*pueblo* league' is the prime example.

For years scholars and jurists have debated the substantive basis of this guarantee to the *pueblos* of New Mexico of one league from a central point — often the village church — in each of the cardinal directions, a measurement not common to all of New Spain. In central Mexico, the territorial norm for Indian *pueblos* was six hundred varas (1 vara = 0.836 metres); Indian villages in most of Nueva Galicia received one-half league (1 league = 4,179.5 metres) in each direction.[37] Why and when indigenous villages in New Mexico were first granted a full league remains hazy. It is clear, however, that by the early

---

[34] See Joaquín Escriche, *Diccionario razonado de legislación y jurisprudencia* (Paris, 1869), pp. 528–9.

[35] See Levaggi, *El virreinato rioplatense en las vistas fiscales de José Márquez de la Plata*, pp. 189, 370, and *passim*. In the face of Bourbon regalist policies that undermined the influence and economic clout of the church, lawyers for the church supported their arguments with appeals to custom, an indication that this still was a legitimate legal point. See D.A. Brading, *Church and State in Bourbon Mexico: The Diocese of Michoacán, 1749–1810* (Cambridge, 1994), pp. 213–4.

[36] The term consensual hegemony is an adaptation of Antonio Gramsci's social theory of cultural hegemony, in which he posited that dominant cultures or ideologies allowed sufficient input from below to afford to all a sense of belonging to the whole. On the application of Gramsci's ideas to scholarship, see Walter L. Adamson, *Hegemony and Revolution: A Study of Antonio Gramsci's Political and Cultural Theory* (Berkeley, 1980). Elaborations of the idea of cultural hegemony include T. J. Jackson Lears, 'The Concept of Cultural Hegemony: Problems and Possibilities', *American Historical Review*, vol. 90 (June 1985), pp. 567–93; Raymond Williams, 'Base and Superstructure in Marxist Cultural Theory', *New Left Review*, vol. 82 (November–December 1973), pp. 3–16.

[37] On the regional variations, see Wistano Luis Orozco, *Los ejidos de los pueblos* (1914; reprint, Mexico City, 1975), pp. 59–72.

eighteenth century, colonial society in New Mexico recognised the legitimacy of these territorial boundaries. While Spanish conceptions of municipal boundaries may have laid the foundations for this measurement, it was the repeated *pueblo* insistence that Spaniards live up to the 'rules of the game' that helped inscribe this territorial dimension as the norm in New Mexico.[38] In 1704, for instance, two Hispanic settlers petitioned for farmland along the Río Grande near San Felipe *pueblo*. Significantly, the petitioners argued that the land in question lay outside the *pueblo* league and thus should be available for settlement.[39] Similarly, during the decade of the 1780s, the natives of both Santa Clara and San Ildefonso *pueblos* found themselves in litigation with encroaching Hispanic *vecinos*. The successful legal strategy of the natives rested on pushing Spanish authorities to reaffirm the guarantee of a full league.[40] Like indigenous subjects elsewhere in the Spanish colonial world, then, the *pueblos* used the legal system as a venue for negotiation and thereby helped in some way to establish the legal norms of the colony.[41]

Another significant, though more subtle, form of judicial custom lay in the way that frontier magistrates acquired and passed on their judicial expertise. In an area that lacked formal education of any kind, transmission of judicial knowledge occurred in an informal manner.[42] They learned by doing. Having gained an elementary education in the home, the sons of the frontier literati began their juridical formation in early adulthood in a most practical way. Felipe Tafoya, for example, served in various official capacities in New Mexico and gained considerable experience in legal affairs, serving in later years as both a magistrate and as a self-styled legal representative (*procurador*). Tafoya and his cohort of local public servants formed the backbone of provincial administration, and they proved to be an indispensable source for staffing the king's judiciary.[43]

---

[38] Discussed more fully in Charles R. Cutter, 'El indio fronterizo ante la justicia española: la creación de una hegemonía consensual', in *IX Congreso del Instituto Internacional de Historia del Derecho Indiano: Actas y Estudios* (Madrid, 1991), vol. 2, pp. 19–28.

[39] SANM I:78, 'Pleyto de Xp.al Xaramillo con los Yndios de S Ph.e', 26 February 1704. The petition was denied by Governor Diego de Vargas.

[40] SANM I:1351, 'Autos Seguidos por los Yndios del Pueblo de S.n Yldefonso contra los Erederos de Juana Luján de fran.co Gómez deel Castillo', 4 February 1763. SANM I:1354, Las Repúblicas de Santa Clara y San Yldefonso to Governor Juan Bautista de Anza, Santa Fe, 6 May 1786. See also, Myra Ellen Jenkins, 'Spanish Land Grants in the Tewa Area', *New Mexico Historical Review*, vol. 47 (April 1972), pp. 113–34.

[41] Among the numerous other examples of recognition of the *pueblo* league are ARAG Civil 267-17-3654, 'El Común y Pueblo de Cochití diciendo de nulidad a la venta de un Rancho cituado en su fundo legal, y reclamando la usurpación de otro', 6 September 1816; SANM I:703, Felipe Sandoval to governor, 17 August 1814; SANM I:1339, 'Petizion a fauor de los Yndios teguas contra Ynacio de Roybal', 16 September 1704.

[42] Oakah L. Jones, Jr., *Los Paisanos: Spanish Settlers on the Northern Frontier of New Spain* (Norman, London, 1979), pp. 55–7 and 136–9, points to the absolute lack of primary schools in Texas and New Mexico until the end of the eighteenth and beginning of the nineteenth centuries. Neither province boasted institutions of higher learning.

[43] For more on Felipe Tafoya, see Cutter, *Legal Culture of Northern New Spain*, pp. 87–8.

These provincially-trained magistrates had in their repertoires the accumulated judicial expertise and practice of previous generations. The authority of legal instruments such as wills and testaments depended on strict compliance with prescribed formulas. And, when dealing with this *derecho privado*, frontier magistrates took care to retain the solemnity of language and form that such documents required. The sphere of *derecho público*, however, proved to be much more fluid. In the vast peripheries of New Spain, the crown permitted local magistrates to resort to simplified criminal and civil procedure, relying mainly on 'known truth and good faith kept'.[44] The so-called *juicio sumario*, which dispensed with the 'solemnities of the law', thus became the usual procedural form in much of the colonial world.[45] In turn, the cumulative judicial 'style' of a local magistracy — always tempered, of course, by crown administrators — became the established method for dispensing justice.

Just as custom formed a crucial ingredient in the legal culture of New Spain, so too did the notion of *equidad* for the common good. Because of the non-adversarial nature of the legal system, the primary aim of the judiciary was to provide justice, not to determine courtroom winners and losers. In a corporatist world where unbridled individualism was not a virtue, the ideal of community wellbeing took precedence over personal gain. Magistrates consistently exercised their *arbitrio judicial* to push for compromise and harmony between contending parties — solutions that, implicitly, conformed to community expectations of fairness.

Consider the case of Antonio de Cárdenas, a New Mexican who had worked for Juan Luján from 1728 to 1732 at a salary of six pesos a month. When the latter died, Cárdenas sought to collect an unspecified amount in back pay from the heirs of Luján. Unsuccessful in this endeavour, he turned to the provincial governor, Gervasio Cruzat y Góngora, as '*padre de pobres*' to rectify the situation. The judicial decision of Cruzat is noteworthy. After reviewing the paperwork, the governor observed that nowhere in the *expediente* was there a contract stipulating the terms of employment. By *law*, the plaintiff had no case. Nevertheless, Governor Cruzat y Góngora ordered the heirs to pay Cárdenas.[46] Although not stated explicitly, *equidad* surely figured in this decision.

---

[44] Quote from ARAG Civil 261-15-3564, 'El común del pueblo de Cochití', f. 95. Archival holdings in Mexico City and in Guadalajara indicate that the crown routinely permitted this simplified form throughout New Spain. See Cutter, 'La magistratura local', *passim*. For central Mexico, see María del Refugio González and Teresa Lozano, 'La Administración de Justicia', in Woodrow Borah (coordinador), *El gobierno provincial en la Nueva España, 1570–1787* (Mexico City, 1985), pp. 77, 78, 83.

[45] On the juicio sumario or extraordinario, see Juan Sala, *Ilustración del derecho real de España* (Valencia, 1803), vol. 2, lib. 3, tít. 2; Pedro Carrillo Sánchez, *Prontuario alfabético de legislación y práctica* (Madrid, 1840), p. 158; Alvarez, *Instituciones de derecho Real de Castilla y de Indias*, lib. 4, p. 212.

[46] SANM II:369, 'Pleyto y demanda q.e puso Antonio de Cárdenas contra los herederos de Juan Luxan sobre los salarios q se le deuian', 5 June–11 September 1732.

Did magistrates in New Spain's far north fully appreciate the role of *equidad* in the construction of *derecho indiano*? Apparently, some did. In deciding a case that involved 'indecorous language', for example, Governor Joaquín Codallos y Rabal observed that the defendant had used 'none of the five [words] deemed to be gravely offensive in law'. Codallos nevertheless specifically invoked equidad (*ussando de equidad*) and condemned the man to pay court costs of ten pesos.[47]

Aptly illustrating the emphasis on community harmony is an incident that occurred at Chama, New Mexico, in 1745. Juan Antonio Salazar and Manuel Valerio, neighbours who also happened to be relatives, had come to a disagreement over that most precious of resources, water. After considering the matter, the provincial governor ordered his lieutenant to urge the two men to meet publicly to settle their dispute. Both would have a right to the water. Lawsuits such as this, reasoned the magistrate, were not only costly but they created 'other pernicious consequences, which between relatives and neighbours are scandalous'. For the sake of community harmony, the governor urged the two to pardon one another and to reach an amicable agreement that neither would break 'in deed or in word, now or forever'. And so they did. The litigants 'embraced one another, and they agreed on the disputed matter in most admirable fashion'.[48]

A magistrate's concern for community harmony might be found not only in urging conciliation at various stages of a legal dispute, but also at the time of pronouncing sentence. The *arbitrio judicial* exercised by local officials at this critical juncture often reflected the values of the Hispanic community. Offenders who disrupted community tranquility and who overstepped the bounds of acceptable behaviour might find themselves excluded from the group. In Texas, New Mexico, and throughout the Hispanic world, crimes such as adultery or fornication often resulted in banishment.[49] In San Antonio, for example, Juan José Vergara — twenty-five years of age, unmarried, 'español' — and María Carbajal had carried on an illicit relationship for years. Although unmarried, the union had produced 'one or two' children and had continued despite official warnings. As custodian of public morality, *alcalde ordinario* José de la Santa took it upon himself to proceed judicially against the wayward couple. After determining that this 'scandal' harmed the community. Alcalde Santa sentenced Vergara to be banished for two years from within forty leagues of the

---

[47] SANM II:465, 'Queja que dio Antonio Baca Alc.e may.r y cap.n a Guerra del Pueblo de Xemes y su Juridicion, contra Hernando Chabez ambos Vecinos de la V.a de S.n Phelipe de Alburquerque sobre hauerle probocado con palabras indecorosas en la forma que adentro se percive', 12–25 June 1745. According to the *Novísima Recopilación de Castilla* 12.25.1, the prohibited words were 'gafo ó sodomético, ó cornudo, ó traidor, ó herege, ó á muger que tenga marido, puta'.

[48] SANM II:465c, 'Causa criminal, a pedimento de Juan Antonio Salazar, contra Manuel Valerio, ambos vecinos de la Villa de Santa Cruz de la Cañada, sobre una herida que le hizo, y malos tratamientos de palabras, en la forma que adentro se contiene', 31 July–6 September 1745.

[49] Illuminating the peninsular viewpoint is José Berní y Catalá, *Práctica criminal* (Valencia, 1749), pp. 7–8, 16.

villa. The woman received not the 'punishment she deserve[d]', but only a warning because, as the alcalde noted, her husband was about to return to San Antonio after a twelve-year absence. In the future the woman was to 'live in appropriate seclusion and modesty' and to maintain a good reputation.[50] A forced reconciliation with a seemingly negligent husband may appear odd to twentieth-century sensibilities, but it fit the patriarchal ideal of proper order in the family that eighteenth-century *tejanos* shared with the Hispanic world.

Considerable evidence indicates that colonial subjects not only expected authorities to take appropriate action to stop improper behaviour, but also that community members themselves often became direct agents of the system by requesting specific punishments or judicial solutions. The participation of *pueblo* groups has been indicated above, and other examples abound. In 1781, for instance, the brothers and uncles of Ana María Trinidad Games appeared before Governor Domingo Cabello requesting that he impede the imminent marriage of the woman to a mission Indian. Although the woman was a '*mulata*', the men believed that a union with Urbano Ynojosa would reflect poorly on the entire family. The plaintiffs must have recognised the likelihood that Cabello would maintain the existing social barriers that hindered racial intermarriage. Indeed, Cabello seemed to display sympathy for the potential injury to one's prestige that such a social mismatch might yield. Before a judicial decision, however, the Games-Hernández clan dropped the suit when Ynojosa declared formally that he wished to marry an Indian woman from the mission rather than Ana María Trinidad Games. In this particular case, the visions of patriarchy and monarchy coincided, and the system worked to uphold the prescribed social order.[51]

To maintain harmony, the law had to provide not only for elites but also for subordinate members of society. They, too, held certain expectations of the legal system. Seeking redress for their grievances, for example, two *genízara* servants complained in 1763 of mistreatment to New Mexico Governor Tomás Vélez Cachupín.[52] The judicial investigation revealed that their Spanish masters had not only neglected to provide properly for the two women but also had failed to instruct them in the Christian faith. Furthermore, one of the servants had been raped while in the fields

---

[50] Béxar Archives (BA), r. 14, fr. 921, proceedings against Juan José Vergara, 4 February–30 June 1782.

[51] BA r. 14, fr. 800, José Miguel Sales Games, Francisco Sales Games, Pedro Hernández and Carlos Hernández v. Urbano Ynojosa and Ana María Trinidad Games, 4 June–29 November 1781.

[52] The *genízaros* of New Mexico were indigenous peoples, usually of Plains origin, who had been captured, traded for or bought by Spanish settlers and served as labourers in a variety of capacities. Over time, many *genízaros* became Hispanicised and, by the end of the eighteenth century, formed important communities located on the frontier of the province. See Fray Angelico Chavez, 'Genízaros', in Alfonso Ortiz (ed.), *Handbook of North American Indians* (Washington, D.C, 1979), vol. 9, pp. 198–200. For a recent assessment of the role of the *genízaros*, see Russell M. Magnaghi, 'The Genízaro Experience in Spanish New Mexico', in Ralph H. Vigil, Frances W. Kaye, and John R. Wunder (eds.) *Spain and the Plains: Myths and Realities of Spanish Exploration and Settlement on the Great Plains* (Niwot, Colorado, 1994), pp. 114–30.

tending sheep (a task deemed unsuitable for women). In his decision, the governor at once ameliorated the plight of the servants and reminded the 'betters' of the responsibilities that accompanied their station. He removed the two servants from under the care of their negligent masters and placed the women in homes 'where they might be instructed in the Christian doctrine and customs and be fed and clothed through household chores appropriate to their sex'.[53]

For Antonia Lusgardia Hernández, an unmarried '*mulata libre*', Texas Governor Manuel de Sandoval embodied the judicial idea of '*protección de los pobres*', and in 1735 she appealed to him for the return of her young son, Ignacio. Eight or nine years previously, explained Hernández, she had entered the household of Miguel Núñez Morillo as a servant. She had left, however, because of her master's mistreatment and negligence in clothing her properly, taking with her two infants — 'one that I brought into the house of said don Miguel, the other that I gave birth to in his house'. Now, she claimed, Núñez and his wife, doña Josefa Flores, had taken the younger child from her 'for no other reason' than because he had been born at the house and because the wife had seen to his baptism. Hernández noted also that Ignacio was 'the only man I have, whom I expect to provide for me as time goes by'. When questioned by the governor, Núñez responded that Ignacio had returned to the household of his own accord. Nevertheless, the couple was willing to return the lad to his mother and serve as his godparents. Satisfied with the outcome, the governor closed the case.[54]

In the preceding examples, and in a striking number of other cases, provincial magistrates used their judicial discretion to find solutions that met the expectations and upheld the contemporary values of the community. We need not overly romanticise the notion of community, for embedded within its construction are ideals that reflect an eighteenth-century Hispanic view of society. At times these contrast sharply with late twentieth-century Western values of individualism and self-realisation.

Conclusions

This, then, was the legal culture that royal subjects had helped forge in the New World, a set of assumptions and expectations about the law that many colonials shared. Distant in time and imbued with a different ideological perspective, some aspects of the Spanish colonial legal system may well seem curious to the modern observer. But the system had a logic of its own, and it appears to have met the needs of the time and to have functioned reasonably well. Rather than revealing malfeasance, capriciousness or ignorance, the record indicates that magistrates in Spanish America usually drew from the ap-

---

[53] SANMII:574, 'Diligencias seguidas por querella de dos yndias genízaras sirbientes contra sus amos', 12–15 October 1763.
[54] BA r. 8, fr. 369, Antonia Lusgardia Hernández v. Miguel Núñez Morillo, 9 August 1735.

propriate sources of *derecho indiano.* If provincial magistrates relied less on *doctrina* and law than their counterparts in the metropolis, they still acted squarely within the Hispanic legal tradition and relied on what they perhaps knew best — custom and *equidad* — in attempting to mete out justice.

The mechanism of *arbitrio judicial* allowed magistrates to respond to community needs and sensibilities, and it provided a way for colonial society to help define the judicial norms of a given area. In a sense, law and *doctrina* afforded a strong and durable framework for generalised judicial administration throughout the empire, while local custom and *equidad* proved to be the fabric from which colonial society elaborated distinctive regional variations. This vulgarisation process — an interplay of royal will and popular sensibilities — was fundamental to the colonial legal system. Rather than a corruption of justice, however, it often served as a legitimate expression of popular values. The vitality of *derecho vulgar* underscores the flexibility of the Spanish colonial law and forces us to reconsider the common perception that the legal system was inherently inefficient, corrupt and irrelevant to the mass of society.

As the nineteenth century dawned, new circumstances — Enlightenment thought, the French Revolution, Bourbon heavy-handedness at imposing the royal will, the political crisis of the Spanish monarchy — all conspired to destabilise the legal culture of the colonial world just as they delegitimised the *antiguo régimen.* Upon achieving independence, the fledgling nations of Spanish America faced the difficult task of rethinking the assumptions that underlay their legal culture and elaborating appropriate systems of law that might achieve congruence between new political paradigms and old social realities.

CHAPTER 2

Colonial Lawyers, Republican Lawyers and the Administration of Justice in Spanish America

Víctor M. Uribe

A few years ago, as I undertook research on the social history of New Granada's colonial and postcolonial lawyers, one of my earliest leads came from
Frank Safford's monograph concerning Colombia's difficulties in training
engineers in the nineteenth century. He showed that this and other regions'
colonial elites had been predominantly inclined to engage in literary, philosophical and legal studies, along with bureaucratic careers, rather than
manual activities. In line with this, he cited an interesting document from
the late eighteenth century produced by a renowned *fiscal* of New Granada's *audiencia*. The *fiscal* complained of the 'excessive' number of lawyers
and demanded that the crown impose strict controls and restrictions on the
further graduation of law students.[1] I consulted the document in question,
and confirmed that during the 1770s Fiscal Moreno y Escandón had indeed
been quite critical of the local Dominican university's generosity with law
students. In his opinion, the university's loose enforcement of graduation
requirements led to a supposed glut in the lawyers' professional market.[2] I
also found that other contemporary bureaucrats complained about there
being too many lawyers in the viceroyalty.[3]

Further research indicated, however, that a few decades after Fiscal
Moreno's complaints, lawyers were considered to be quite scarce. David
Bushnell, in his work on state-building during General Santander's early
(1821–27) post-colonial regime, for instance, quoted New Granada's parliamentary debates of 1823 and 1824 that alluded to the lack of lawyers.
Members of Congress, cited by Bushnell, pointed out that the implemen-
tation of the new republican administration of justice was being hindered
by the lack of sufficient attorneys to fill positions within the judicial system,
provided for in the country's new constitution and laws. The primary

---

[1] Frank R. Safford, *The Ideal of the Practical: Colombia's Struggles to Train a Technical
Elite* (Austin, 1978), p. 88. The document has also been cited approvingly by Thomas Blos-
som, *Nariño: Hero of Colombia's Independence* (Tucson, 1967), p. xvii.
[2] Francisco Antonio Moreno y Escandón, 'Documento sobre el Exceso de Abogados' [1771],
Documentos Biblioteca Luis Angel Arango (Bogotá, 1771).
[3] For another primary document alluding to the inconvenient abundance of lawyers see
Francisco Silvestre, *Descripción del Nuevo Reyno de Granada* (Bogotá, 1968) [1789], p. 116.

sources quoted by Bushnell and others, such as the minutes of Colombia's 1820s *consejo de gobierno*, confirmed the existence of such a problem.[4]

Was there a contradiction between the arguments and some of the pieces of evidence uncovered by those two American authors and myself? Probably not. It might have been the case that the size of the legal profession declined dramatically between the late colonial and the early independence period. To dispel any contradiction one could also argue that some circumstances of the late colonial state did make the number of lawyers seem excessive; and that the size of the legal profession in existence at the opening of the post-colonial period appeared dwarfed relative to the expanding requirements of the republican bureaucracies, particularly the new justice system. It is also possible that the alleged excess of colonial lawyers or the supposed abundance of republican ones were incorrect. If either one or a combination of the above circumstances could not be established, then, probably, there was a contradiction after all.

Shedding light on this seeming discrepancy might help to elucidate some aspects of the social and political history of Colombia and other regions. Lawyers were not only a key segment of colonial and post-colonial society, but were also active participants in the process of state building. Furthermore, they were a controversial group. Whether there were many or very few of them, in different periods, could thus contribute to explaining both the shape of Spanish American societies, and some aspects of the process of state building in this region, including the state's capacity to overhaul the justice system. Even particular social behaviour and attitudes towards, for example, manual labour and litigation, may also be better understood by looking at this issue, for their abundance might have exemplified the elites' disdainful attitudes toward manual trades. These attitudes and behaviour will not be explored here though. For the present the emphasis will be on politics and state building.

The first two parts of this chapter address some of the above queries. They focus not only on New Granada, but also touch on the epicentres of the other three viceroyalties in existence in the late colonial period: namely New Spain, Peru and Río de la Plata. These places all witnessed, like New Granada, the debate on the abundance of colonial lawyers, and in some of them there is also evidence that the scarcity of republican lawyers was lamented in the first half of the nineteenth century, and caused problems for justice administration. These two sections are mainly dedicated to demographic and political aspects. The final section of this chapter provides a general discussion of justice administration in some regions

---

[4] David Bushnell, *The Santander Regime in New Granada* (Newark, 1954), p. 37; Roberto Cortázar and Luis Augusto Cuervo (eds.) *Congreso de 1823. Actas* (Bogotá, 1926), p. 167. For other primary sources indicative of the scarcity of attorneys available to take charge of judicial posts in the 1820s see *Acuerdos del Consejo de Gobierno de la República de Colombia*, 2 vols., 2nd. ed. (Bogotá, 1988).

during both the colonial and early republican period. In addition to comparing the evolution of judicial institutions, it demonstrates that, probably because of the dissimilarities as to the formation of legal experts in each colonial region, Spanish and Portuguese America followed opposite paths when it came to deciding how to arrange postcolonial judicial institutions.

Finally, though the original intention was to discuss the postcolonial era, the periodisation used here results from my conviction that to make sense of most issues in nineteenth-century Latin America (especially the first half), it is essential to examine simultaneously this century along with the colonial period and the period of Independence.[5]

Colonial lawyers in Latin America

Unlike the United States or England, apprenticeship with established attorneys was not enough in colonial Latin America to become a lawyer. Formal education culminating in an academic degree (whether it be *bachiller, licenciado,* or *doctor*) was indispensable. By the late eighteenth century the numerous centres of higher education scattered throughout the colonial landscape had produced hundreds of such law graduates.[6] Having completed the rest of the requirements — practical training and some exams — many of these law graduates subsequently became lawyers and registered

---

[5] Some prefer to refer to this longer period as the 'age of democratic revolutions'. See R. R. Palmer, *The Age of Democratic Revolution: Political History of Europe and America, 1760–1800,* 2 vols. (Princeton, 1959–1964); Eric J. Hobsbawm, *The Age of Revolution [Europe], 1789–1848* (London, 1962). On its significance see also Woodrow Borah, 'Discontinuity and Continuity in Mexican History', *Pacific Historical Review* 48 (February, 1979), pp. 1–25; Eric Van Young, 'Mexican Rural History Since Chevalier: The Historiography of the Colonial Hacienda', *Latin American Research Review* XVII, 3 (1983), pp. 5–61; and 'Recent Anglophone Scholarship on Mexico and Central America in the Age of Revolution (1750–1850)', *Hispanic American Historical Review,* vol. 65 (1985), pp. 725–43 (742); Mark D. Szuchman (ed.), *The Middle Period in Latin American History. Values and Attitudes in the 18th and 19th Centuries* (Boulder: Lynne Reiner Publishers, 1988), esp. pp. 11–13, 18. For recent research see Jaime E. Rodríguez, *Mexico in the Age of Democratic Revolutions, 1750–1850* (Boulder, 1994); Mark D. Szuchman and Jonathan Brown (eds.), *Revolution and Restoration. The Rearrangement of Power in Argentina, 1776–1860* (Lincoln, 1994); Kenneth J. Andrien and Lyman L. Johnson, *The Political Economy of Spanish America in the Age of Revolution, 1750–1850* (Albuquerque, 1994).

[6] See María Rodríguez C. Agueda, *Historia de las universidades hispanoamericanas,* vol. 1 (Bogotá, 1973). Lanning indicates that nine universities were opened in colonial Spanish America before even one college was established in English America. See John Tate Lanning, *Academic Culture in the Spanish Colonies* (Oxford, 1940), p. 3. Still, by 1775 most US lawyers learned their craft by serving as apprentices to established lawyers, and only 150 Americans had received formal training at the Inns of Court in London. Brazil's first law schools were created in the late 1820s. See Jerome Reich, *Colonial America,* 3rd ed. (New Jersey, 1994), p. 183; Charles R. McKirdy, 'The Lawyer as Apprentice: Legal Education in Eighteenth–Century Massachusetts', *Journal of Legal Education,* vol. 28 (1976), pp. 124–36, esp. 124–6; E. Bradford Burns, *A History of Brazil,* 3rd ed. (New York, 1993), pp. 115, 146.

themselves to practice within one of the several *audiencia* (court) districts.[7] As time went on, local lawyers, along with a diverse gamut of other formally educated individuals or *letrados*, came to be essential components of Spanish America's colonial landscape.[8] Furthermore, besides the locally trained, there were also lawyers from Spain itself, for whom numbers are not available, who continued to migrate regularly into the colonies. This body of experts, local and European alike, reflected the nature of colonial society and served essential functions required by both society and the state.

Male elites (whites, 'old Catholics', legitimately born, from noble or wealthy families of non-manual workers) and some upwardly mobile ones (sons of middling bureaucrats and provincial landowners or merchants, and a meagre number of mixed race individuals), chose or were selected by their families to be trained in the law. Law degrees, and subsequent admission to the register of the *audiencia's* lawyers, became a way to gain individual and familial prestige, the means to a respectable occupation, or the credentials for a yet more 'honourable' and convenient undertaking: serving the state. Late colonial law graduates turned out to be a mixed bag including: (1) relatively affluent non-practising individuals dedicated to more profitable ventures such as mining, ranching, and trade; (2) practising professionals earning usually modest incomes which, along with other family endeavours, allowed them, nonetheless, to maintain their elite status or even gain upward mobility; and (3), bureaucrats of various ranks. The latter aspired to move up the bureaucratic ladder and enter into convenient family alliances to enhance their individual and familial status, honour, economic wellbeing and power.[9] In addition, because of overlaps in their training ('canon law'

---

[7] Thirteen different *audiencia* districts were created throughout the colonial period. The first was established in Santo Domingo in 1511. The last in Cuzco in 1787. See Mark Burkholder, 'Bureaucrats', in Susan Socolow and Louisa S. Hoberman (eds.), *Cities and Society in Colonial Latin America* (Albuquerque, 1986), pp. 77–103.

[8] See Angel Rama, *La ciudad letrada* (Hanover, 1984), p. 27. I thank John Chasteen for making me aware of the importance of Rama's work, a translation of which he is currently preparing. The word *letrado* came to be particularly associated with the legal professionals.

[9] Evidence of the above mentioned social background, occupations and status of colonial lawyers can be found in *Abogados del Ilustre Colegio de la Excma Ciudad de Lima* (Lima, 1813), pp. vii–xix; Carlos A. Luque Colombres, *Abogados en Córdoba del Tucumán* (Córdoba, 1943); Ricardo Levene, *Historia del derecho argentino* (Buenos Aires, 1946), vol 2, pp. 461–3, vol 3, 411–75; also 'Notas para la historia de los abogados en Indias', in *Revista Chilena de Historia del Derecho*, vol. 1 (1959), pp. 9–12; Vicente Osvaldo Cutolo, *Abogados y escribanos del siglo XVII* (La Plata, 1963); Atilio Cornejo, 'Abogados de Salta', *Revista del Instituto de Historia del Derecho Ricardo Levene*, vol. 21 (1970), pp. 210–303; Miguel Angel de Marco, *Abogados, escribanos y obras de derecho en el Rosario del siglo XIX* (Rosario, 1973); Vicente Oddo, *Abogados de Santiago del Estero durante el primer siglo de existencia de la ciudad (1553–1653)* (Santiago del Estero, 1981); Víctor M. Uribe, 'Lawyers and New Granada's Late Colonial State', *Journal of Latin American Studies*, vol. 27, part 3 (October 1995), pp. 517–49. For claims that lawyers did not come from the aristocratic circles see John Kicza, 'The Legal Community of Late Colonial Mexico: Social Composition and Career Patterns', in Ross Hassig and Ronald Spores (eds.), *Five Centuries of Law and Politics in Central Mexico* (Nashville, 1984), pp. 127–44. Opposite views are expressed in Joel R. Poinsett, *Notes*

being a substantial component of the priestly and legal curriculum), a fair number of lawyers were also members of the priesthood.[10]

Besides their most obvious technical roles in counselling and litigation, late colonial lawyers played various other functional roles in colonial Latin America. These were mainly the mainenance and enhancement of familial and individual status, and bureaucratic and ecclesiastical service. All of this benefited both the influential and middle segments of society, the church, and the state itself. Furthermore, these lawyers were also active in the local city councils or *cabildos,* and served as college professors. Notwithstanding their social position and numerous services to society, to some officials and civil observers lawyers became an inconvenience because of their supposedly high numbers.

The 'excessive' number of *abogados*

In late colonial New Spain (Mexico) contemporary observers bemoaned the 'crecido número de pleitos' caused by the abundant number of *procuradores* (solicitors), *escribanos* (scribes), *relatores* (notaries) and, particularly, *letrados* or lawyers. Lawyers, in particular, were abhorred due to the fact that they made a living ('comen, beben y triunfan') at the expense of peoples' patrimonies ('a costa de los caudales y bienes ajenos'). Consequently, it was demanded that 'la mano poderosa del gobierno' reduce the number of attorneys. Despite the opposition of the local Colegio de Abogados and the reports of several *intendentes,* who argued that more lawyers rather than fewer were actually necessary, the Real Audiencia was specially charged by the crown with impeding the registration of new ones.[11] In early nineteenth-century Río de la Plata the authorities also enacted legislation to curtail the number ('combatir el incremento') of lawyers. In 1802 and 1803, strict measures were passed to regulate the exact number of lawyers (i.e., 24 maximum in Buenos Aires, eight in cities which were capitals of an *inten-*

---

on Mexico Made in the Autumn of 1822 (New York, 1969), p. 121. That the typical lawyer was neither rich nor a member of a prominent family but a man of modest means is a thesis put forward in P. Michael McKinley, *Pre-Revolutionary Caracas. Politics, Economy and Society, 1777–1811* (Cambridge, 1985), pp. 134–6. On legal careers as an instrument of social mobility see also Tulio Halperín Donghi, *Politics, Economics and Society in Argentina in the Revolutionary Period* (Cambridge, 1975), p. 49.

[10] These were devoted to either the administration of affluent parishes and personal fortunes, or the performance of clerical functions within the ecclesiastical bureaucracy which, much like the civil one, was also abundant and prestigious. See Uribe, 'Lawyers and New Granada's Late Colonial State'.

[11] Hipólito Villaroel, *Enfermedades políticas que padece la capital de esta Nueva España* [1785–1787] (México, 1982), pp. 123–30; Hans W. Baade, 'Número de abogados y escribanos en la Nueva España, la provincia de Texas y la Luisiana', in *Memoria del III Congreso de Historia del Derecho Mexicano* (México, 1984), p. 121. The Guadalajara *audiencia* also lamented in 1805 la *'falta de letrados'* throughout New Galicia's provinces. See Del Arenal Fenochio, 'Los abogados en México y una polémica centenaria', in *Revista de Investigaciones Jurídicas,* vol. 4 (1980), p. 545.

dencia, six in other cities).[12] Similarly, in New Granada, and all of the *dominios de Indias*, including Peru, bureaucrats and other observers requested that the number of *abogados* be reduced, as it was seen as excessive. The crown went on to tighten up the standards for graduation and augmented the years of practical training prior to becoming an *audiencia* lawyer.[13] Despite these eyewitness observations and contemporary measures, other historical evidence from these regions may help to ascertain whether or not lawyers were as numerous as was being charged. This, in turn, will permit us to see if perceptions about their inconvenience derived from demographic or from other more pressing factors.

A late eighteenth-century (1785–87) observer indicated the number of lawyers in the capital of New Spain to have been approximately 175, probably more if one counted *los de residencia foránea*.[14] Contrary to other contemporary reports that listed a total of 210 lawyers in the viceroyalty, reliable secondary sources have estimated membership in New Spain's 1804 Colegio de Abogados (the Mexico *audiencia* district, excluding New Galicia or the Guadalajara *audiencia*) to have been 258, most of whom (207, some 80 per cent) resided in Mexico City. There were but a few in other places. For example, 23 in Puebla, four in Veracruz, and three in San Luis Potosí.[15] New Spain was then a region with an estimated population of close to six million. Based on these sources and figures, a valid estimate of the number of lawyers in this viceroyalty gives us between 180 and 270 in the late colonial period. There may, however, have been as many as 300 to 350 lawyers in total, if one includes New Galicia (the Guadalajara *audiencia* and its environs).[16] That is to say a rather optimistic grand total of 0.5 lawyers per 10,000 inhabitants.

Contemporary calendars listed around 130 lawyers in New Granada.[17] Based on other sources, I have elsewhere estimated the total to have been

[12] Levene, *Historia del derecho argentino*, vol. 2, pp. 461–3.

[13] Francisco Silvestre, *Descripción del Reyno de Santafé* [1789] (Bogotá, 1968). On the rest of Spanish America, Peru included, see Del Arenal Fenochio, 'Abogados de México', pp. 535–6; Ricardo Levene, *Historia del derecho argentino* (Buenos Aires, 1951), vol. VI, p. 462. On new restrictions see Uribe, 'Lawyers and New Granada's Late Colonial State'.

[14] Villaroel, *Enfermedades políticas*, p. 129.

[15] Kicza, 'The Legal Community of Late Colonial Mexico', pp. 127–44. The Colegio de Abogados de México reported that there were 210 in 1805. See Hans W. Baade, 'Número de abogados y escribanos', pp. 119–28. An 1807 list refers to 312 lawyers. See María del Refugio González, 'El ilustre y real Colegio de Abogados de México frente a la Revolución Francesa', in Alberto Solange et al. (eds.), *La Revolución Francesa en México* (Mexico, 1992), pp. 111–35.

[16] An 1805 report from the Guadalajara *audiencia* referred to around 43 lawyers in the district of the *audiencia*. See Jaime del Arenal Fenochio, 'Los abogados de México', pp. 544–5. On population estimates see Timothy E. Anna, *The Mexican Empire of Iturbide* (Lincoln, 1990), p. 50.

[17] Antonio García de la Guardia, *Kalendario manual y guía de forasteros para el año 1806* [1806] (Bogotá, 1988). A list of the lawyers registered in late colonial Audiencia de Caracas included over 110 names. At least a few of these, though, were also in New Granada's count (e.g., Casimiro Calvo, Francisco Garcia Hevia, Frutos Gutiérrez, Jacinto Ramírez). The combined total of lawyers for New Granada and Venezuela may not have exceeded 230. See the

up to 150 lawyers in the late colonial period. At least half of them resided in Bogotá, the rest were scattered all over the region.[18] New Granada was then a region of nearly 1,100,000 people, which would mean a ratio of 1.3 lawyers per 10,000 inhabitants.

A directory of the Viceroyalty of Peru in the late eighteenth century (1793) listed just 50 lawyers in the city of Lima. This was doubtless an incomplete estimate, since some authors refer to census data listing 91 lawyers in late colonial Lima.[19] A calendar for the year 1813 lists a seemingly more accurate figure: 177 law graduates in the entire Viceroyalty of Peru. Two years later the lists included 203.[20] Relying on these sources, it is fair to estimate the lawyers of late colonial Peru to have been between 150 and 200. Considering that the population of this viceroyalty in about 1800 was 1,100,000 (excluding Quito, and Charcas or present Bolivia with Potosí), the ratio of lawyers was approximately 1.6 per 10,000 inhabitants.

According to some secondary sources, in the late colonial period (c. 1785–1802) there were 98 lawyers registered in the Buenos Aires *audiencia*. 54 were registered between 1802 and 1811, resulting in a combined total of 152 lawyers in the early nineteenth century.[21] A valid estimate for the late colonial period points to some 100 to 170 lawyers in the Viceroyalty of Río de la Plata. This was then a region of 440,000 inhabitants (encompassing what is now Paraguay and Uruguay), which indicates a ratio of 3.4 lawyers per 10,000 inhabitants.

These statistics, though imperfect given the fragmentary and incomplete nature of some of the sources, nonetheless give us an approximate ratio of lawyers per inhabitant in several colonial regions. The area with the most abundant supply of lawyers per 10,000 inhabitants was Río de la Plata with twice as many lawyers as the next region, namely Peru. Peru was followed closely by New Granada, and in a far distant fourth place was Mexico where there were fewer than half as many lawyers as in New Granada or Peru, and seven times fewer than in Argentina. Therefore, although in absolute terms Mexico had the largest number of lawyers, followed by Peru, New Granada, and Argentina, relative to their population the sequence was the exact opposite.

Caracas colonial list in Héctor Parra Márquez, *Historia del Colegio de Abogados de Caracas*, 2 vols. (Caracas, 1952), vol 1, pp. 399–402.

[18] Uribe, 'Lawyers and New Granada's Late Colonial State', pp. 517–49.

[19] Hipólito Unanue, *Guía política, eclesiástica y militar del Virreinato del Perú para el año de 1793* [1793] (Lima, 1985), pp. 58–63. The calendar left blank the spaces for the list of lawyers in the city of Cuzco, and failed to mention those of other urban centres such as La Plata and Arequipa. The source listing 91 lawyers is Alberto Flores Galindo, *Aristocracia y plebe. Lima, 1760–1830 (estructura de clases y sociedad colonial)* (Lima, 1984), p. 71.

[20] *Abogados del Ilustre Colegio*, pp. vii–xix.

[21] Levene, 'Notas para la historia de los abogados en Indias', pp. 9–12.

Table 1. Lawyers in Some Areas of Late Colonial Latin America by Region and Population.

Region	Year	Number	Population (c. 1800)	Ratio* per 10,000 people
New Spain	1787	175 (Mexico City)	5,837,000	
	1804	258 (New Spain)		
	1805	300–350 (+ New Galicia)		0.5
Peru	1793	50 (Lima)	1,100,000	
	1790s	91 (Lima)		
	1811	177		1.6
New Granada	1806	130–150	1,100,000	1.3
Río de la Plata	1785–1802	98	440,000	
	1802–1811	54 (additional)		
	1785–1811	152		3.4

Sources: Villarroel, *Enfermedades políticas*, p. 129; Uribe, 'Lawyers and New Granada's Late Colonial State'; Levene, 'Notas para la historia de los abogados en Indias', pp. 9–12; Kicza, 'The Legal Community of Late Colonial Mexico', pp. 127–44; Abogados del ilustre Colegio, pp. vii–xix; Flores Galindo, *Aristocracia y plebe*, p. 71; James Lockhart and Stuart B. Schwartz, *Early Latin America* (Cambridge, 1983), p. 338. *The ratio has been calculated based on the highest possible number of lawyers.

Notwithstanding the above demographic differences, and the claims of at least a few contemporary observers and even state officials regarding the need for more lawyers, representatives of the late colonial state argued that the number of lawyers all over Spanish America was excessive.[22] Consequently, they took measures to curtail it everywhere. However abundant the number of lawyers in the Spanish colonies may have ultimately seemed to the crown, it pales when compared to the number of attorneys present in late eighteenth- and early nineteenth-century France, England or the United States.

For example, in 1789, there were 276 practising 'barristers' in Tolouse, France. This city alone, thus, had as many lawyers as the entire Viceroyalty of New Spain and almost twice as many as New Granada or Río de la Plata.[23] Paris had as many as 712 lawyers in 1738, and an average of 540 lawyers between 1700 and 1789. Again, this was more than double the figure for any colonial viceroyalty in Spanish America.[24] The English bar,

---

[22] For contemporary claims that more lawyers were needed see Baade, 'Número de abogados', p. 121; Del Arenal Fenochio, 'Los abogados de México', p. 545.
[23] See Lenard R. Berlanstein, *The Barristers of Toulouse in the Eighteenth Century (1740–1793)* (Baltimore, 1975), p. 12.
[24] See David A. Bell, *Lawyers and Citizens. The Making of a Political Elite in Old Regime France* (Oxford, 1994), p. 28.

considered 'one of the smallest professions', had no fewer than 1,000 members in the late eighteenth century and almost 2,500 by the 1830s. This 'small profession' was, therefore, five to seven times larger than any of the bars in the Spanish colonies.[25] As for the United States, both the northern and southern states had many more lawyers than any individual region of Spanish America. There were, for example, 24 lawyers for every 10,000 residents in 1775–90 Massachusetts. The number had increased to 70 by 1810 and 87 by 1820. In South Carolina, there were 19 per 10,000 in 1771 and the number had jumped to 40 per 10,000 by 1820.[26] The United States, thus, had regions with from 6 to 30 times more lawyers than the most attorney-dense Spanish American colony.

Clearly, the active judicial and political life of cities such as Toulouse or Paris, and the thriving economies of France, England and the United States, afforded more abundant business to some of those lawyers than to their ordinarily work-hungry Latin American colleagues who inhabited economically modest or depressed regions. Be that as it may, the truth seems to be that the number of Spanish American lawyers may not have been comparatively as excessive as contemporary authorities claimed.

Lawyers were, nonetheless, definitely considered 'too numerous' by several state officials in late colonial Spanish America. More importantly, they were deemed contrary to public order. Why was this so? Excessive lawyer-driven litigation could have been, as contemporary observers in New Granada and New Spain argued, a valid reason.[27] But litigation was not new. It had been intense since the sixteenth century and there is no evidence of an extraordinary increase meriting special reactions or measures in the late colonial period.[28] Furthermore, it seems that in Spain, where lawyers were also about to fall under attack for their allegedly excessive number, litigation was actually on the decline in the late eighteenth century.[29] Therefore, excessive litigation does not seem a powerful enough

---

[25] See Daniel Duman, *The English and Colonial Bars in the Nineteenth Century* (London, 1983), pp. 1–7.

[26] James Henretta and Gregory Nobles, *Evolution and Revolution. American Society, 1600–1820* (Lexington, 1987), p. 216.

[27] See Villarroel, *Enfermedades políticas*, pp. 123–30; See Pedro M. Carreño, 'Atavismo litigioso', *Boletin de Historia y Antiguedades* [hereafter BHA], vol. 31, no. 355–6 (1944), pp. 556–62; Alejandro B. Carranza, *Don Dionisio de los Caballeros de Tocaima* (Bogotá, 1941), p. 221.

[28] Scattered evidence on the intensity of colonial litigation can be found in Steve Stern, *Peru's Indian Peoples and the Challenges of Spanish Conquest* (Madison, 1982); Woodrow Borah, *Justice by Insurance: the General Indian Court of Colonial Mexico and the Legal Aides of the Half-Real* (Berkeley, 1983); Susan Kellogg, *Law and the Transformation of Aztec Culture, 1500–1700* (Norman, 1995); Beatriz Patiño, *Criminalidad, ley penal y estructura social en la Provincia de Antioquia, 1750–1820* (Medellín, 1994); and Victor M. Uribe, 'Rebellion of the Young "Mandarins": Lawyers, Political Parties, and the State in Colombia, 1780-1850', unpublished PhD thesis (University of Pittsburgh, 1993).

[29] On litigation in Spain during the colonial period see Richard L. Kagan, *Lawsuits and Litigants in Castile, 1500–1700* (Chapel Hill, 1981), esp. p. 237. Similar works are lacking for Spanish America.

reason to explain anti-lawyer sentiments in Iberia and its colonies. There might, then, have been other more powerful motives.

Lawyers' inconvenient activities and expectations

Pre-revolutionary and revolutionary events and circumstances might afford some more compelling reasons to explain the crown's stand against lawyers. These events and circumstances suggest that alleged 'revolutionary' activities on the part of lawyers and other intellectuals, and their active role at abetting what today we may call an embryonic 'public sphere of civil society', were probably among the real reasons for containing the growth of this profession and moving to regulate training more closely.[30]

During the late 1780s and early 1790s, elite plots were uncovered in, for example, Minas Gerais, Rio de Janeiro, Santafé de Bogotá, Mexico City, la Guaira, and even in Madrid itself. In several such plots lawyers were leading figures.[31] The crown soon moved against the participants in the plots in question, which indicated its apprehension over any suspicious activities among 'enlightened' individuals, lawyers included. The crown's repressive reaction also hints at its weariness over the penetration, however limited, of republican ideals in the colonies and over the beginning of a 'civil public sphere', a space of intellectual debate and critique.[32]

---

[30] On the public sphere see J. H. Habermas, *The Structural Transformation of the Public Sphere* (Cambridge, 1994); Benjamin Nathaus, 'Habermas's "Public Sphere" in the Era of the French Revolution', *French Historical Studies*, vol. 16 (1990), pp. 620–41. For an interesting discussion of how Habermas's 'public sphere' emerged within civil society as a counterpart to public authority see Dena Goodman, 'Public Sphere and Private Life: Toward a Synthesis of Current Historiographical Approaches to the Old Regime', *History and Theory*, vol. 31, no. 1 (1992), pp. 1–20.

[31] See Emilia Viotti da Costa, *The Brazilian Empire. Myths and Histories* (Chicago, 1985), pp. 5, 9, 11; Carolyn E. Fick, *The Making of Haiti: The Saint Domingue Revolution from Below*, (Knoxville, 1991), esp. Chapter 3; Germán Pérez Sarmiento, *Causas célebres a los precursores: 'Derechos del Hombre', pesquisa de sublevación, pasquines sediciosos. Copias fieles y exáctas de los originales que se guardan en el Archivo General de Indias* (Bogotá, 1939), vol. 1, pp. 497–9; See Michael C. Meyer and William L. Sherman, *The Course of Mexican History* (New York, 1991), pp. 278–9; John Rydjord, 'The French Revolution in Mexico', *Hispanic American Historical Review* (1929); Hugh Hamill Jr., *The Hidalgo Revolt. Prelude to Independence* (Gainesville, 1966), p. 9; Richard Herr, *The Eighteenth-Century Revolution in Spain* (Princeton, 1958), pp. 325–6; McKinley, *Pre-Revolutionary Caracas*, pp. 134–6. There was a popular revolt in 1798 Bahia allegedly also inspired by French revolutionary ideas. See Katia de Queiros Mattoso, *Presença francesa no Movimiento Democrático Bahiana de 1798* (Salvador, 1969).

[32] On the repercussions of the French Revolution in Spain and its colonies see Robert M. Maniquis et al. (eds.), *La revolución francesa y el mundo ibérico* (Madrid, 1989); Ricardo Krebs and Cristian Gazmuri (eds.) *La revolución francesa y Chile* (Santiago de Chile, 1990); Alberto Solange et al. (eds.), *La revolución francesa en México* (México, 1992); and Joseph K. Klaits and Michaerl H. Haltzel (eds.), *The Global Ramifications of the French Revolution* (Cambridge, 1994), especially pp. 158–76; and, François Xavier Guerra, 'Revolución francesa y revoluciones hispánicas: una relación compleja', in his *Modernidad e independencias. Ensayos sobre las revoluciones hispánicas* (Madrid, 1992), pp. 19–54.

In addition to having participated in plots, lawyers contributed to developing new institutions for social interaction (clubs, cafes, salons, academies, lodges, philanthropic associations, *tertulias* and so on) which made it possible for individuals to gather, rationalise, criticise and ultimately try to mould 'public opinion' and influence the state's policies.[33] Furthermore, they were active in the establishment of a permanent press in the 1790s and early 1800s — a press which, of course, was in part founded with the support and encouragement of enlightened officials of the colonial state.[34]

Along with their penchant for gregarious activities, and the new literary and journalistic endeavours, because of the nature of their training, lawyers were the most likely intellectuals to be aware of current 'revolutionary' doctrines on government, sovereignty and legislation. These were ordinarily taught in the classes of '*derecho de gentes*', '*derecho natural*' and 'public law' introduced, both in Spain and some colonies in the second half of the eighteenth century.[35]

---

[33] See J. Jaramillo Arango, 'Don José Celestino Mutis y las expediciones botánicas españolas del siglo XVIII al Nuevo Mundo', *Revista de la Academia Colombiana de las Ciencias Exactas, Físicas y Naturales*, vol. 9 (1958); Thomas F. Glick, 'Science and Independence in Latin America (with Special Reference to New Granada)', *Hispanic American Historical Review*, vol. 71, no. 2 (1991), pp. 307–34; Herr, *Eighteenth-Century Revolution*, Chapter 6; Jean Serrailh, 'Les sociétés Economiques de Amis du Pays', in *L'Espagne éclairée de la seconde moitié du XVIII siécle* (Paris, 1964), pp. 223–85; Mariano García Ruipérez, *Nuevas aportaciones al estudio de las sociedades económicas de Amigos del País* (Madrid, 1988). On the creation of public-interest societies in New Granada see Margarita Garrido, *Reclamos y representaciones*, p. 44. For other regions (e.g., Veracruz, Lima, Santiago de Cuba, La Habana, Guatemala, Quito) see F. de las Barras Aragón, 'Las sociedades económicas en Indias', *Anuario de Estudios Americanos*, vol. 12 (1955), pp. 417–47; R. J. Shafer, *The Economic Societies in the Spanish World (1763–1821)* (Syracuse, 1958); and Felipe Barreda y Laos, *Vida intelectual del virreinato del Peru* (Buenos Aires, 1973).

[34] See José Toribio Medina, *Historia de la imprenta en los antiguos dominios españoles de América y Oceania*, 2 vols. (Santiago de Chile, 1958); Henry Lepidus, 'The History of Mexican Journalism', *University of Missouri Bulletin*, vol. 29, no. 4 (January 1928), pp. 20–1; Guerra, 'La difusión de la modernidad: alfabetización, imprenta y revolución en Nueva España'; Renán Silva, *Prensa y revolución a finales del siglo XVIII* (Bogotá, 1988); Garrido, *Reclamos y representaciones*, pp. 45–9; Noble David Cook, 'Education and the Leaders of Peruvian Independence', in Francisco Miró Quesada et al. (eds.), *Historia, problemas y promesa*, 2 vols. (Lima, 1978), vol. 1, pp. 63–88, esp. pp. 66 and 69; Félix Denegri Luna, 'Apuntes para un estudio bibliográfico de la Gaceta del Gobierno (1823–1826)', in *Gaceta del Gobierno del Perú* (Caracas, 1967), vol 1, pp. lxiii–c; Juan Rómulo Fernández, *Historia del periodismo argentino* (Buenos Aires, 1943), p. 39; José Durand, 'Prologo', in Hipólito Unanue, *Guía política, eclesiástica y militar*, pp. ix–xxxiii; Simon Collier, *Ideas and Politics of Chilean Independence, 1808–1833* (Cambridge, 1973), p. 271; Hilda Sabato, 'Citizenship, Participation and the Formation of the Public Sphere in Buenos Aires 1850s–1880s', *Past and Present* (August, 1992), p. 151 and p. 163; Víctor Uribe 'Lawyers and the Emergence of the "Public Sphere of Civil Society" in Spanish America During the "Age of Revolution", c. 1780s–1850s', unpublished manuscript, 1996.

[35] In Spain these works were introduced in the 1770s and in some of the colonies by the early 1790s. See Herr, *Eighteenth Century Revolution*, pp. 173–83; Víctor M. Uribe, 'Disputas entre estado y sociedad sobre la educación de los abogados a finales de la etapa colonial en la Nueva Granada', *Historia y Sociedad*. Revista del Departamento de Historia, Universidad

Finally, perhaps more important than all of the above, was the fact that local lawyers were also active in performing 'public' or 'civic' roles in the city councils (*cabildos*), and were fit and all too eager to pursue bureaucratic activities. The *cabildos* competed with the royal bureaucracy over control of local affairs, including the regulation of weights and measures, food supply, licensing of stores and other businesses, allocation of lands and so forth. They also wrestled with royal bureaucrats over honour and precedence. In addition, the *cabildos'* predominantly creole members, who belonged to influential local clans and family networks, led to petitions to the crown for more participation by Americans in the high levels of state bureaucracy. Some such petitions were drafted by *cabildo asesores*, that is lawyers who, much as the rest of their peers, were traditionally avid seekers of bureaucratic positions, particularly coveting the honour of becoming *oidores* and *fiscales* in the *audiencias*, the highest courts within the Spanish colonies.[36]

Of the different state agencies, the *audiencias* were, in fact, the only really attractive 'judicial' bodies that lawyers might have been eager and glad to join.[37] The other 'judicial' posts (*alcaldes mayores* and *alcaldes de la Santa Hermandad*, and *corregidores*) were more numerous and less difficult to obtain, but much less attractive than a position in an *audiencia*. As there were just thirteen courts in the entire colonial period, each with but a few seats for judges (*oidores*) and prosecutors (*fiscales*), the competition for *audiencia* appointments was fierce and difficult. It became even more difficult in the second half of the eighteenth century when the crown introduced new restrictions on the participation of creole aspirants.[38]

Neutralising lawyers became, thus, important on several accounts: under the guise of aiding a reduction in litigation it would help to curtail diverse threats of political subversion and serious bureaucratic pressures. In Spain itself soon after the French Revolution, and despite evidence that lawyers were not contributing to any increase in litigation, royal decrees began to be enacted to limit the number of lawyers in Madrid and to tighten up the requirements for graduation. This happened in 1794.[39] This chapter has already noted the complaints and measures in the colonies against lawyers from Mexico to Argentina during the 1790s and early 1800s. Together with

Nacional de Colombia, Medellin (1996); Cook, 'Education and the Leaders of Peruvian Independence', p. 65. On the importance of the teaching of *derecho natural* in late eighteenth-century Spain see François Xavier Guerra, 'Imaginarios y valores de 1808', in *Modernidad e independencias*, pp. 149–75, esp p. 170.

[36] See Mark Burkholder and Dewitt S. Chandler, *From Impotence to Authority: The Spanish Crown and the American Audiencias, 1687–1808* (Columbia, 1977); Mark Burkholder, *Politics of a Colonial Career: José de Baquijano and the Audiencia of Lima* (Albuquerque, 1980).

[37] The *audiencias* were not strictly only judicial bodies, but also acted as 'administrative' councils.

[38] See Burkholder and Chandler, *From Impotence to Authority*; and Burkholder, *Politics of a Colonial Career*.

[39] See Ley XXX, tit. 22, lib. 5, *Novísima recopilación*. On evidence of decreasing litigation, including José Covarrubias's 1789 *Discurso sobre el estado actual de la abogacia en los tribunales de la nación*, see Kagan, *Lawsuits and Litigants*, pp. 237–46.

restrictions on the number of lawyers to be allowed in the peninsula and the colonies and harsher standards for graduation (i.e., a longer period of practical training), the Spanish crown proceeded to prohibit in both places the teaching of the new doctrines of public law and *derecho natural y de gentes*, and emphasised instead the need to teach royal legislation (*derecho real*).[40] Moreover, by 1802 the crown had introduced in some colonies special officials (*censores regios*) to censor any potentially subversive doctrine in law schools and elsewhere.[41] Thus occured an assault on legal education and lawyers, an assault which was accompanied by the diffusion of the soon-to-be generalised belief that there were too many lawyers.

The number of lawyers was not excessive, after all. It was their activities and skills which, in an era of turmoil, preoccupied the crown. The fact that different colonial voices began to complain of this profession's 'excessive' number of members, was thus very likely a reflection of the political climate of the late colonial era rather than the product of a real demographic problem. The troubling political events in the colonies and the Iberian peninsula seem to have made the Spanish authorities particularly eager to contain, and closely oversee, the further training of a potentially subversive generation of young intellectuals. These had demonstrated organising skills, abilities in public critique and debate, and were, again, likely to become easily acquainted with, and help diffuse, anti-royal legal theories; namely, the new constitutional doctrines springing from the American and French Revolutions.

Years later, though many were rather conservative at heart, lawyers proved the crown more or less right. They undertook journalistic endeavours and became active in organising all sorts of revolutionary committees. They would also mould, legitimate and design the constitutions that accompanied Spanish America's revolutionary movements and the establishment of new polities.

The revolutionary days

There is some evidence, however, of the highly conservative attitudes of the majority of lawyers, both in Spanish America and elsewhere.[42] Even in France where members of this profession — particularly Parisian lawyers — were massively involved in the ideological struggles that helped bring the Revolution about, had an overwhelming presence (46 per cent of the total) among the deputies of the Third Estate convened in Versailles in May 1789, and rallied *en masse* to the patriot party, there is recent research indicative

---

[40] Herr, *Eighteenth-Century Revolution*, pp. 173–6, 371–3.
[41] On the establishment of *censores reales* to eliminate 'doctrina alguna contra la autoridad y regalias de mi corona' see 'Temores de Fernando VII', *Boletín de Historia y Antigüedades*, vol. 7, (1912), pp. 704–6; Juan M. Pacheco, *La ilustración en el Nuevo Reino de Granada* (Caracas, 1975), pp. 102–3. See also Uribe, 'Disputas entre estado y sociedad sobre la formación de los abogados'.
[42] See Uribe, 'Lawyers and New Granada's Late Colonial State'.

of lawyers' deep-seated conservatism.[43] Nevertheless, much as the alleged plots uncovered during the 1790s seem to have had the active participation of some local *letrados* (priests, teachers, and lawyers), members of the legal profession, sometimes seemingly as a conservative manoeuvre, also became active during the movement for independence in Spanish America.

The active role of lawyers in the relatively early and forceful independence movements of Río de la Plata and New Granada is widely acknowledged. Lawyers actively participated in the *cabildo* meetings that unleashed these revolts, and took part in the revolutionary committees and governments themselves. More than half of the members of the *cabildo* of Buenos Aires May 22, 1810, for instance, were lawyers and only one voted against the removal of the local viceroy. No wonder that a little later, the local *audiencia* judges claimed that they had been removed from their jobs by local *abogados revoltosos.*[44] Three such lawyers, Manuel Belgrano and Juan Martín de Pueyrredón from the elite, and the upwardly mobile Mariano Moreno, subsequently played leading public functions in the republican period.[45] In New Granada, as I have demonstrated elsewhere, numerous lawyers also sat in the *cabildo* that removed the viceregal authorities, and subsequently played dominant roles in government and society.[46]

Much less is known about lawyers' participation in the ultimately reluctant independence of both Mexico and Peru. It seems that, as with these regions' mercantile and mining elites (to whose families some of them belonged), lawyers, even those active in the emerging 'public sphere', rather than advocating revolution, were generally favourable to the monarchy.[47] They, therefore, contributed to maintaining the elite unity that generally characterised such countries and served to delay independence. Of course, a few of them from the 'lesser creole class' did join early, but ultimately fruitless, revolts. Such was, for instance, the case of Bernardo Chico Valdés (Jose María Chico?), son of a Guanajuato *regidor*, who

---

[43] For regional research on the conservative attitudes of attorneys in pre-revolutionary France, contrary to what authors such as Alfred Cobban and Georges Lefebvre had argued, see Lenard Berlanstein, *The Barristers of Toulouse*, especially Chapter 6; and Michael P. Fitzsimmons, *The Parisian Order of Barristers and the French Revolution* (Cambridge, 1987). Yet some recent works considered lawyers to have been 'midwives' of the new, critical 'public politics' that arose in France over the course of the eighteenth-century, waging a permanent public campaign against despotism in the crown and church. See Bell, *Lawyers and Citizens*, p. 8.

[44] Levene, *Historia del derecho*, vol 2, p. 466.

[45] Osvaldo Vicente Cutolo, 'Los abogados en la Revolución de Mayo', *Tercer Congreso Internacional de Historia de América* (Buenos Aires, 1961), vol. 5, pp. 199–212; Ricardo Levene, 'La historia de los abogados en el Río de la Plata y su intervención en la Revolución de Mayo', *Revista Jurídica Argentina La Ley* 41 (January-March, 1946), pp. 911–22.

[46] See Victor M. Uribe, 'Kill all the Lawyers! Lawyers and the Movement for Independence in New Granada, 1809–1820', *The Americas*, vol. 52, no. 2 (October 1995), pp. 175–210.

[47] Flores Galindo, *Aristocracia y plebe*, pp. 71–2; David Brading, *Miners and Merchants in Bourbon Mexico, 1763–1810* (Cambridge, 1971), pp. 317–8.

became rebel priest José María Hidalgo's Minister of Justice; and, (Ramón?) Ignacio Rayón, a successful young lawyer from the small locality of Tlalpujahua, who became his secretary-in-chief. Fifty-four-year-old lawyer Miguel Domínguez, a pro-Indian *corregidor* in Querétaro from a seemingly more influential local family, also supported the conspiracy.[48] Similarly, numerous members of Mexico's secret revolutionary society of the Guadalupes were prominent creole lawyers.[49] In Peru, a fair number of lawyers, even those from elite families, would join the independence movement in due course, with seemingly conservative designs.[50]

Lawyers, in sum, organised and sat in revolutionary committees, funded progressive associations (e.g., *sociedades patrióticas* and *sociedades económicas*), and agitated in the streets or the classroom.[51] Furthermore, during the revolutionary transition, they guided the process of institution building and restructuring. They oversaw the suppression of colonial institutions, drafted constitutions and legislation, and devised new tribunals and state agencies.

As a result of their revolutionary political activism and journalism, lawyers were targeted by the Spanish repression. In regions like Colombia, a quarter of them were executed in the years after 1810. In Mexico several were also persecuted, exiled, and even executed. This can be presumed to have also occurred in Río de la Plata and Peru, though research on this matter is still sparse.[52] In any event, it is fair to say that the ranks of the profession, which were already limited, were further depleted during the independence period due to repression. To compound the situation, numerous royalist Spanish lawyers fled from Spanish America. Furthermore, the disruption of educational activities caused by the Wars of Independence probably impeded the graduation of enough new local lawyers. All of these factors thus brought about a decrease in the size of the legal profes-

---

[48] See Brading, *Miners and Merchants*, p. 344; Hamill, *The Hidalgo Revolt,* pp. 106, 144, 147, 169.

[49] Such lawyers included Nicolás Becerra, Manuel Díaz, José Ignacio Espinoza, José María Falcón, José Benito Guerra, José María Llave, José Matoso, Juan Nazario Peimbert and Antonio del Rio. See Timothy E. Anna, *The Fall of the Royal Government in Mexico City* (Lincoln, 1978), p. 119; Wilbert H. Timmons, 'Los Guadalupes: A Secret Society in the Mexican Revolution for Independence', *Hispanic American Historical Review*, vol. 30, no. 4 (November, 1950), pp. 453–99; Virginia Guedea, *En busca de un gobierno alterno: Los Guadalupes de México* (México, 1992). See also del Refugio González, 'El Ilustre y Real Colegio de Abogados', pp. 111–35.

[50] Cook, 'Education and the Leaders of Peruvian Independence', p. 75.

[51] On the creation of revolutionary associations, lodges and societies during the 1810s see Pilar González Bernaldo, 'Produccción de una nueva legitimidad: ejército y sociedades patrióticas en Buenos Aires entre 1810 y 1813' in *Cahiers des Amériques Latines*, vol. 10 (1990), pp. 177–95; José A. Ferrer Benimelli, 'Bolívar y la Masonería', *Revista de Indias*, vol. 43, no. 172 (July–December 1983), pp. 631–78; Shafer, *Economic Societies*; L. E. Fisher, 'Early Masonry in Mexico (1808–1826)', *Southwestern Historical Quarterly*, vol. 42, no. 3 (1939); J. A. Mateos (ed.), *Historia de la Masonería en México desde 1806 hasta 1884* (Mexico, 1884).

[52] Uribe, 'Kill all the Lawyers!'. Fragmentary information on the Mexican case can be found in González, 'El Ilustre y Real Colegio de Abogados de México', p. 119.

sion. The establishment of a new system of technically trained judges in the post-colonial period was likely to be hindered by this circumstance.

Having interpreted late colonial claims and measures against the 'abundance' of lawyers as the result of political expediency, and suggested that the number of lawyers in Spanish America might have declined due to political repression and other circumstances during the 1810s, it is fair to conclude that at the outset of the post-colonial period lawyers were less abundant that one might have expected. The administration of justice in post-colonial Latin America probably suffered due to this problem.

Lawyers and justice in Spanish America.

In colonial Latin America some justice was administered by lay people, including royal functionaries without any legal training.[53] For instance, criminal justice was in the hands of the *alcaldes ordinarios*, the *corregidores* and their lieutenants, the late eighteenth-century (*gobernadores*) *intendentes* (and their *subdelegados*), and a few special tribunals like the tribunales de la Santa Hermandad. Some of these bodies (*alcaldías mayores* and *alcaldes de la Santa Hermandad*), were scattered throughout the viceroyalties and were staffed by individuals of notable local families elected annually by the local city councils. They were generally honorific positions held by laymen without legal training; and were even seen by some as a burden. Some other positions, the *corregimientos* for instance, were also equally scattered within each viceroyalty but were handled by appointees of the local viceroys or the Spanish crown, named on the basis of support from influential patrons, networking by prestigious local families, or the purchase of the appointment by wealthy individuals intent on further increasing their power, wealth and honour. Even though lawyers occasionally held such jobs, *Corregidores* were not required to belong to the legal profession.[54]

Of course, there were other more specialised and technical courts, like Mexico's General Indian Court, its late colonial Tribunal de Acordada, the tribunales del consulado, and, of course, the Royal *audiencias*.[55] *Audiencia*

---

[53] See Chapter by Cutter in this volume.

[54] See Colin M. MacLachlan, *Criminal Justice in 18th Century Mexico: A Study of the Tribunal of the Acordada* (Berkeley, 1974); Ulises Rojas, *Corregidores y justicias mayores de Tunja y su provincia desde la fundación de la ciudad hasta 1817* (Tunja, 1962).

[55] On the General Indian Court, a specialised body with alternate jurisdiction in suits of Indians with each other and in those of Spaniards against Indians, see Borah, *Justice by Insurance*. The Tribunal de Acordada, which grew out of the 'hermandad' to police certain rural crimes like banditry and traffic in illegal liquors, was presided by a lay judge assisted on a regular basis by both *letrados* and several officials with defined functions. See MacLachlan, *Criminal Justice in 18th Century Mexico*. On the merchant-staffed Tribunales del Consulado, charged with the resolution of mercantile disputes, see Julio César Gillamondegui, 'Notas para el estudio de la justicia mercantil patria en las provincias argentinas', *Revista del Instituto de Historia del Derecho*, vol. 20 (1969), pp. 117–34. On colonial justice in general see also, among others, Edberto Oscar Acevedo, 'Notas sobre la administración de justicia en la

positions, the most significant for our discussion, were fairly centralised, and were staffed by a mixture of political appointees or wealthy buyers, and career bureaucrats, normally all of whom were lawyers.[56] In fact the *audiencia* positions were, as I mentioned above, lawyers' most coveted positions, as they carried substantial salaries, power and social prestige. The other 'judicial' positions were only rarely held by lawyers. Though some such positions (*corregimientos*) were valued for the power, money and influence that they might accrue to their holders, these jobs were seen mostly as temporary stepping-stones on the long road to reaching the greatness of an *audiencia* job.

Since it was willing to allow local lay people to preside over them, the crown did not seem to have minded also letting creole lawyers handle several of the different institutions involved in justice administration at the local level. As for the *audiencias*, however, Mark Burkholder and Dewitt S. Chandler have ably demonstrated that, during the second half of the eighteenth century, the crown wanted to regain exclusive control of these courts by peninsular appointees.[57] Intent as it was on refurbishing its colonial bureaucracy by appointing peninsulars and excluding members of local society, the crown became especially weary of lawyers' demands for participation in this level of government. It is no surprise, therefore, that during the revolutionary period, at least in Río de la Plata and Nueva Granada, lawyers soon moved against the *audiencias*. In the process, they also ended up overhauling the entire judicial system.

In Río de la Plata and Nueva Granada the revolutionaries expelled the Spanish *oidores*, refurbished and renamed the *audiencias*, the clearest symbols of late colonial oppression. They even abolished colonial dress codes for court judges and lawyers, which were seen as symbols of the past. In Argentina, for example, under the leadership of the Jacobin attorney Mariano Moreno, the *rioplatenses* eliminated the *audiencias'* ceremonial and dress codes.[58] Then they undertook the separation of judicial and other functions, a separation which had been foreign to the colonial state that had traditionally combined within the same organs what post-

---

intendencia de Salta', *Revista del Instituto de Historia del Derecho*, vol. 9 (1958), pp. 57–82; Patiño, *Criminalidad, ley penal y estructura social*; Tamar Herzog, *La administración como un fenómeno social: La justicia penal de la ciudad de Quito (1650–1750)* (Madrid, 1995); Charles Cutter, *The Legal Culture of New Spain* (Albuquerque, 1995).

[56] José M. Restrepo, *Biografías de los mandatarios y ministros de la Real Audiencia (1671–1819)* (Bogotá, 1952); Guillermo Lohman Villena, *Los ministros de la Audiencia de Lima en el reinado de los Borbones (1700–1821): esquema de un estudio sobre un nucleo dirigente* (Sevilla, 1974); Ali López Bohórquez, *Los ministros de la Real Audiencia de Caracas, 1786–1810: caracterización de una élite burocrática del poder español en Venezuela* (Caracas, 1984).

[57] See Burkholder and Chandler, *From Impotence to Authority*; Mark Burkholder, *Politics of a Colonial Career: José de Baquijano and the Audiencia of Lima* (Albuquerque, 1980).

[58] Following the expulsion of the Spanish *oidores*, in Buenos Aires the revolutionary decree of June 22, 1810, drafted by radical lawyer Mariano Moreno, abolished the 'traje y solemnidades imperantes' in the former *audiencias*. See Levene, *Historia del derecho*, vol 2., pp. 465–6.

colonial society would understand to be separate functional spheres: namely judicial, executive, and legislative activities.[59]

As a result of the Reglamento de Institución y Administración de Justicia, enacted in January of 1812 to establish a 'nueva justicia' for 'un pueblo libre', the Río de la Plata's *audiencias* of Charcas and Buenos Aires each became a *Cámara de Apelaciones*. Staffed by local *conjueces*, the *cámaras* in question had 'todas las facultades y atributos que las leyes concedían a las Reales Audiencias'.[60] To reduce the monopoly attorneys held over judicial representation, and probably also to expedite the resolution of cases whenever attorneys were unavailable, it was ordered that any person could act on their own behalf in criminal and civil cases, without being backed by a lawyer.[61] In addition, citizens themselves were made more active in the resolution of local conflicts.

To be sure, a significant degree of participation by lay people in the administration of justice had already existed. The colonies' *alcaldes ordinarios*, prominent local individuals, had been charged with the resolution of judicial cases in the colonial period. But the revolution tried to expand these bodies. In 1812, following in the footsteps of the pre-judicial conciliation attempted after 1791 during the French Revolution, each of Río de la Plata's cities was to have a Tribunal de Concordia, made up of two members of the local city council and the council's *síndico*. This new body was charged with the conciliation of disputes before they turned into law suits. The new philosophy underlying judicial administration was, as far as possible, to 'prevenir contiendas'. As the establishment of these *tribunales* seems to have been delayed for unknown reasons, new measures were introduced to make their creation more pressing. For example, in a Nuevo Reglamento de Administración de Justicia, enacted in September 1813, it was provided that all legal disputes be submitted first to the Tribunal de Concordia, before they could be even tried by the *jueces ordinarios*.[62] Yet, this Nuevo Reglamento also abolished the 1812 provisions allowing indi-

---

[59] See the October 22, 1811 'Reglamento fijando las atribuciones, prerrogativas y deberes de los poderes legislativo, ejecutivo y judicial', cited in Roberto I. Peña, 'La aplicación del derecho Castellano Indiano por los Tribunales Judiciales de Córdoba (1810–1820)', *Revista del Instituto de Historia del Derecho*, vol. 18 (1967), pp. 129–69, esp. p. 138. Such demarcation was still blurred, for governors and their lieutenants were charged to hear judicial appeals. Only in a new 'Reglamento provisorio', dated 3 December 1817, were they finally exempted from judicial functions. *Ibid.*, p. 158.

[60] See Samuel W. Medrano, `Problemas de la organización de la justicia en las primeras soluciones constitucionales', *Revista del Instituto de Historia del Derecho*, vol. 6 (1954), pp. 67–86.

[61] *Ibid.*, pp. 138–43; Miguel Ibáñez Frocham, *La organización judicial argentina (ensayo histórico). Epoca colonial y antecedentes patrios hasta 1853* (La Plata, 1938), pp. 54–7; Luis Méndez Calzada, *La función judicial en las primeras épocas de la independencia* (Buenos Aires, 1944), p. 145. See also Medrano, 'Problemas de la organización de la justicia'.

[62] These were the former *alcaldes ordinarios* who, generally not being legal experts themselves, had to decide the cases in close consultation with *asesores*, who were trained attorneys.

viduals to act without the need for an attorney.[63] Furthermore, the other measures were suspended two years later.

During the so-called Revolución Federal Nacional of 1815, an *estatuto provisional* established a new judicial structure. First, it created a new sort of supreme court, the Tribunal de Recursos Extraordinarios de Segunda Suplicación, Nulidad e Injusticia Notoria, alongside the two *audiencia*-like *cámaras de apelación*. Secondly, it abolished the *tribunales de concordia*, that is the municipal-level conciliation bodies created in 1812 and 1813. Thirdly, it developed a series of guarantees like *habeas corpus*, and the requirements of warrants for searching private houses and it also established the freedom of the press. Finally, the new statute determined that *cabildos* were to be popularly elected, thus also democratising the character of *cabildo*-appointed *jueces ordinarios*.[64]

Continuing with the political and institutional instability characteristic of the 1810s, the new rules were not long-lasting. Further changes took place soon afterward. The attributes of attorneys, which had been curtailed by the 1813 legislation, were conversely expanded. In 1817, they were charged with the role of appellate judges in every province. Lawyers thus replaced the governors and their lieutenants who, contrary to the supposed 'separation of powers' then in place, had continued to perform judicial duties.[65] This began a trend to professionalise justice at the appellate level. This trend, like the other changes, was not merely theoretical but was actually implemented and observed. Evidence concerning the resolution of judicial conflicts in, for example, the province of Córdoba, demonstrates this.[66] However, other changes subsequently introduced in Argentina and elsewhere were hindered by different factors, in particular the lack of attorneys.

In Mexico, just to mention another example before looking at the obstacles that the lack of law professionals soon posed, the changes of the 1810s were less traumatic and radical than those of Argentina. Mexico, similar to Peru, continued to be royalist. Clearly, Mexicans followed the dictates of the 1812 Cádiz Constitution and had to introduce adjustments to the structure of the judiciary. Some such adjustments, much as those being effected in Río de la Plata in late 1811, were geared towards making the judiciary independent from the other two branches of the tripartite constitutional monarchy established in Cádiz. As a result of the attempted separation of functions, *audiencia* judges tried to resist the changes, which would make them lose the power,

---

[63] Ibáñez Frocham, *Organización judicial argentina*, p. 61.

[64] See Peña, 'La aplicación del derecho castellano', pp. 156–7.

[65] See the 'Reglamento provisorio' of 3 December 1817. *Ibid.*, pp. 158–9; Ibáñez Frocham, *Organización judicial argentina*, p. 76. Concerning administration justice in New Granada during the revolutionary period see Jose María Ots y Capdequí, 'The Impact of the Wars of Independence on the Institutional Life of the new Kingdom of Granada', *The Americas*, vol. 17, no. 2 (October, 1960), pp. 111–98, esp. pp. 128–30, 140–7.

[66] *Ibid.* On the functioning and structure of justice in other Argentine provinces during the late 1810s and beyond the 1820s see Ibáñez Frocham, *Organización judicial argentina*, pp. 95–156.

prestige, and economic benefits accruing from their participation in diverse colonial administrative committees and commissions.

Despite the resistance, the *audiencia* of Mexico, and presumably Guadalajara's also, became an appellate court; and its magistrates (the same individuals who had served as the late colonial *audiencia's oidores*) were stripped of non-judicial powers. As it became an appellate court, first instance cases were to be transferred from the former *audiencia* to lower courts. But there were no such courts yet, and the magistrates and civil governor Calleja were reluctant to have neighbourhood creole *alcaldes* (*alcaldes de barrio*) involved in first-instance judicial proceedings in the meantime. Therefore, disobeying some of the provisions of the Cádiz constitution, the *audiencia*-turned-appellate court continued to act as court of first instance. Furthermore, the transformation of the *audiencia* was reversed in late 1814 when the traditional colonial order was re-established and the *audiencia* and its judges resumed business as usual.

In the spring of 1820, however, the Cádiz Constitution was reestablished and the ministers proceeded to reintroduce the recently reversed changes turning *audiencias*, once more, into appellate courts with exclusively judicial duties. This time, as opposed to their actions of 1812, they somewhat democratised first-instance justice. They authorised Mexico City's thirty-two neighborhood *alcaldes*, and all of the *intendencias'* legal advisors and subdelegates, to serve as first-instance judges until technically trained 'district judges' could be appointed.[67]

In late 1821, applications for district judgeships started to be received. But, much like the creation of a 'supreme court of justice', badly needed to preside over an independent judicial branch and solve the backlog of cases in the appellate court, the appointment of district judges and the creation of a national judiciary were delayed until a Constituent Congress met in 1823.[68]

The Congress kept the appellate courts and created a new Federal Supreme Court. The members of this new court, reflecting some decentralising forces then in vogue, were to be appointed by Congress itself on the basis of lists of candidates submitted by each of the federation's states. Once they were appointed, the members of the court proceeded to ask qualified lawyers to apply for positions on eight new 'circuit courts' and 21 new 'district courts'. They ranked the applicants and sent the lists to the executive. But a major problem arose in filling the positions: the limited supply of qualified lawyers. Due to the lack of lawyers to take over the jobs 'half of the [eight] circuit courts did not begin to function for several more years', and it is fair to assume that similar difficulties hindered the func-

---

[67] See Linda Arnold, *Bureaucracy and Bureaucrats in Mexico City, 1742–1835* (Tucson, 1988), pp. 60–6.

[68] *Ibid.*, pp. 75–7. See also Lucio A. Cabrera 'History of the Mexican Judiciary', *Miami Law Quarterly*, vol. 11, no. 4 (Summer 1957), pp. 439 48.

tioning of the almost two dozen new district courts.[69] As it was being pro-
fessionalised, personnel shortages hampered the establishment of the new
judicial system in 1820s Mexico. Argentina and Colombia, and probably
other regions, soon faced similar difficulties.

The 1820s witnessed attempts by several Spanish American republics to
establish a professional judiciary. Of course, as had occurred in the colonial period, most countries continued to have lay municipal and parochial
judges, variously called *jueces ordinarios, jueces pedaneos* or *jueces de
paz.* These were generally unpaid, untrained town-level magistrates,
elected for a year or two to adjudicate petty matters and conciliate pro-
spective litigants. They were thus equivalent to the colonial *alcaldes ordinarios,* charged with the resolution of minor judicial disputes.[70] The
appointment of *letrados* to preside over local and regional judgeships became, however, a pressing matter as time went on. In Buenos Aires, as the
cabildos were suppressed in late 1821, five *juzgados letrados de primera
instancia,* soon to be reduced to four, were created.[71] In Córdoba, Argentina, the *juzgados letrados en lo civil y criminal* were established in 1824.[72]
In 1825, Colombia established the so-called *jueces letrados de primera instancia* and the *jueces letrados de hacienda.* There was to be one of the
former in every municipality, and one of the latter in every province.[73]
The circuit and district judgeships established in 1824 Mexico were also to
be staffed by *letrados.*[74] But *letrados* could not always be found, and the
professionalisation of the judiciary failed to materialise for quite a while. The
problem was compounded by the lack of the necessary funds to pay for the
functioning of the new judiciary. Federalist inclinations, and attempts at establishing a symmetrical judicial bureaucracy in each country's provinces,
'cantons' and municipalities, further aggravated the situation, for it determined the need for more functionaries than merely those who were indispensable in a centralised system. Of these various problems, the lack of
qualified magistrates was quite significant.

In Mexico, personnel shortages hindered the inauguration of the regional judiciaries. The pool of qualified lawyers for the new jobs was quite
limited. Only two of the projected eight circuit courts had been opened in
1828. One more was inaugurated in 1829, and another only in 1830. The
other four, much like the numerous district courts, would have to wait until

---

[69] See Arnold, *Bureaucracy and Bureaucrats,* p. 77.
[70] See Roberto I. Peña, 'Contribución a la historia del derecho patrio en Córdoba: Labor in-
stitucional del gobernador Bustos (1820–1829)', *Revista del Instituto de Historia del Derecho,* vol. 11 (1960), pp. 107–24, esp. p. 115.
[71] Carlos Mario Storni, 'Acerca de la "papeleta" y los juzgados de paz de la campaña bonaerense',
Revista del Instituto de Historia del Derecho, vol. 20 (1969), pp. 153–71, esp. p. 157.
[72] Peña, 'La aplicación del derecho castellano', p. 160.
[73] Bushnell, *The Santander Regime,* pp. 27–8.
[74] Arnold, *Bureaucracy and Bureaucrats,* p. 77.

much later.[75] In Colombia the supply of candidates for judicial office did not match the number of available jobs either. For several years, numerous municipalities and provinces lacked *jueces letrados de primera instancia* or *jueces letrados de hacienda*.[76] In Argentina, the new structure could not be implemented until much later due to the lack of *letrados*.[77] Provincial reports of even the 1850s still alluded to the scarcity of law professionals to take charge of the Tribunales Inferiores a la Corte Suprema de Justicia.[78]

It seems that in all of these Spanish American regions, the few lawyers available were unwilling to abandon the main cities and move to provincial locations. In fact, most practising lawyers lived in or near the capital or other important cities. They preferred to reside in Mexico City and Guadalajara, Bogotá, Córdoba, and Buenos Aires or Lima rather than elsewhere. Appointees to courts in peripheral areas, thus, tended to decline the appointments.[79] The republic would have to lower its expectations of soon having a professional judiciary; or else it would be required to produce lawyers at a faster pace. The latter happened in New Granada, which opened the doors of law schools wide during the 1830s, and validated all kinds of law courses taken by individuals in the numerous provincial high schools established throughout the country.[80] In Argentina by the 1850s, it was decided to expedite the graduation as lawyers of many who had not completed their formal studies or practical training.[81] The cases of Mexico and Peru still await further research.

Conclusions

The lack of attorneys to staff the professional judiciary of the 1820s and beyond is significant for various reasons, which suggest intriguing questions for further research. First of all, it hints at the possibility that the allegedly abundant, even 'excessive', legal profession in Spanish America during the late colonial period must have been a politically-motivated royal myth. This chapter shows this to have been the case. In the second place, such a shortage also suggests that a radical reduction of the size of Spanish America's legal profession probably occurred during the period of independence. Such reduction definitely took place in Colombia, and probably also happened in Mexico, Argentina and elsewhere. More interestingly, the lack of sufficient lawyers may have determined the adoption of corrective measures in the post-colonial period, measures which had

---

[75] *Ibid.*, pp. 77, 166.
[76] Bushnell, *The Santander Regime*, p. 37.
[77] Ibáñez Frocham, *Organización judicial argentina*, p. 172.
[78] See de Marco, *Abogados, escribanos y obras de derecho*, pp. 11–12.
[79] Arnold, *Bureaucracy and Bureaucrats*, pp. 77, 166; Bushnell, *The Santander Regime*, p. 38.
[80] Uribe, 'Rebellion of the Young Mandarins', chapter 6.
[81] De Marco, *Abogados, escribanos y obras de derecho en el Rosario*, p. 12.

unexpected consequences. One such measure — facilitating the graduation of numerous lawyers — probably helped, at least in the medium term,
to establish the new judicial organs created during and after the 1820s.
Yet the presence of an increasing number of lawyers can be presumed also
to have had major unexpected side effects: the expansion of Spanish
America's 'middle sectors' and the strengthening of liberalising tendencies.
These sectors, likely to have had expectations of upward social mobility
and to have embraced liberal ideas, doubtless contributed to the intensifi-
cation of political confrontation with conservative elements; and they
pushed for further political reforms of a liberal nature.[82] What is paradoxical about this lawyer-inspired liberalising and reformist change is that it
resulted from quite the opposite trend to that characteristic of the liberalisation of justice in, say, Portuguese America.

As Thomas Flory has demonstrated, the liberalisation of justice in
1820s and 1830s Brazil resulted from the creation in 1827 of the office of
juiz de paz or justice of the peace. These were untrained, unpaid, local-
level magistrates, elected for a year to adjudicate small disputes and attempt conciliation. They were an expression of the liberals' call for decen-
tralisation, self-government, democratic forms, etc. Quite the reverse of
the crown magistrates' subordination to the monarchy, the *juiz de paz*'s
'independence' was especially valued by the Brazilian liberals.

This 'independence' went against the emperor's traditional position as
supreme arbiter of justice and the source of judicial authority. In sum, the
elective lay judges were seen as an instrument of reform. To be sure, the
liberals were soon to be disenchanted with some of the new magistrates.
Besides elbowing out municipal councils, priests, and militia commanders,
thus becoming too powerful and sometimes abusive, the election of the
new judges was controlled by the dominant social elites and the magistrates often became too dependent on local bosses. Yet, for a number of
years the liberals continued to place their hopes in these local lay judges,
many of whom certainly came from humble stock and possessed the aspirations of the upwardly mobile.[83]

In Spanish America liberal hopes were not placed in the lay judges,
who had been in existence through the colonial period in the form of the
alcaldes ordinarios. Progressive hopes were placed instead on the certainty
and predictability of constitutions and laws, vehicles to avoid personal ar-
bitrariness, applied and sanctioned by professional magistrates or *jueces
letrados*. Furthermore, while in Brazil the liberalising trend which had led
to the ascendancy of lay judges was being reversed in the early 1840s
when, under conservative rule, appointment became the dominant mode

---

[82] On the significance of middle sectors in post-colonial politics see Torcuato di Tella, *National Popular Politics in Early Independent Mexico, 1820–1847* (Albuquerque, 1996).

[83] See Thomas Flory, *Judge and Jury in Imperial Brazil, 1808–1871. Social Control and Political Stability in the New State* (Austin, 1981).

of selection of lesser judges (to be named from among the graduates of Brazil's new legal faculties), in Spanish America these appointed professionals were still then part of the liberal agenda, as they had been since the 1820s. Because there were not enough of them, Spanish American liberals advocated the expansion of legal education to train enough candidates to the magistracy and other public jobs. In doing so, they ended up expanding even further the liberal (provincial, upwardly mobile) ranks and generally deepening liberal reforms. Some also argued that this liberalising trend contributed to much political instability and social tension.[84]

---

[84] Such was the opinion of New Granada's conservative minister, Mariano Ospina R. See his *Esposición que el Secretario de Estado en el Despacho del Interior...Dirije al Congreso Constitucional de 1842.* (Bogotá, 1841), p. 9. On the tensions produced by the traditional social structure developed in the colonial period, and liberal trends in the postcolonial period see Donald Fithian Stevens, *Origins of Instability in Early Republican Mexico* (Durham, 1991).

CHAPTER 3

Privileged Justice? The *Fuero Militar* in Early National Mexico

Linda Arnold

Valerio Salto did not want to die. He had been born in Tiripitio, Michoacán some years before Independence. A local judge in early 1848 had convicted and sentenced him to death for his role in the pillaging of El Mineral de Curucupaseo.[1] Salto appealed the sentence through the first, second and third instances. Denied a sentencing reversal by the appellate court in Morelia on 14 May 1848, he petitioned the governor of Michoacán for a pardon. Denied a pardon yet still seeking further recourse, Salto decided to tell his attorney that he was an army deserter. After his attorney informed the regional military commandant that ordinary jurisdiction courts had convicted and sentenced a deserter, the commandant immediately protested and ordered an investigation to verify Salto's jurisdictional status.

Rebuffed by the civilian authorities who had convicted Salto, the regional military commandant filed a conflict of jurisdiction brief with the Federal Supreme Court. In early national Mexico the Supreme Court decided hundreds of conflicts of jurisdiction.[2] Between 1826 and 1837, less than 30 per cent of conflict of jurisdiction cases involved military courts; the majority involved disputes between different local ordinary jurisdiction courts and between local ordinary jurisdiction and federal jurisdiction courts.[3] Of the seventy conflicts of jurisdiction between ordinary jurisdiction courts and military courts during those years, 21 involved civil plaintiffs and 49 involved criminal defendants. Unlike the brief about the Salto case, in virtually all of the criminal cases either a civilian or a military judge filed his brief shortly after the arrest of a defendant, not after conviction and sentencing. Still, Valerio Salto obviously hoped that subordi-

---

[1] José María Casasola, *Colección de alegaciones y respuestas fiscales, estendidas en varios negocios civiles y causas criminales que se han visto en el Supremo Tribunal de Justicia de la Nación, habiendo entre las últimas algunas bastante celebres*, 2 vols. (México, 1860), vol. 1, pp. 120–41.

[2] Archivo de la Suprema Corte de Justicia [Anexo], Libro 186, Libro de conocimientos o pases de autos al fiscal de esta Suprema Corte de Justicia, 1826–1839. Competencias. For a comprehensive discussion of conflict of jurisdiction jurisprudence, see Manuel de la Peña y Peña, *Lecciones de práctica forense mejicana, escritas a beneficio de la Academia Nacional de Derecho Público y Privado de Méjico* (México, 1835–1839), vol. 1, pp. 194–230.

[3] To consult those briefs, see Linda Arnold, 'Archivo General de la Nación, Galería Cinco, Archivo de la Suprema Corte de Justicia, Catálogo de documentos, 1826 a 1837. Transcripción de un manuscrito con 1150 referencias a documentos localizados en el Archivo General de la Nación' (México, 1988), typescript, 119 pp.

nating himself to the regional military commandant might lead to a new trial, a new round of appeals and reviews, and a different sentence.[4] For a regional military commandant during the spring of 1848 on the other hand, as the US troops withdrew victoriously, reorganising his battalions, pursuing deserters and imposing strict military discipline in a dispirited army were his priority concerns.

Acting on the counsel of his legal advisor, the commandant in Michoacán pursued jurisdiction for Salto's case. He, as with his counterparts throughout the country, had to re-establish his regional authority and contain the rampant problem of desertion. Salto, though, had not deserted during the war or the months of foreign occupation. Rather, drafted in October 1829 for a ten-year tour of duty with the active militia battalion formed in Morelia, Salto first deserted in February 1830. Returning to his battalion after just a few weeks, he deserted again on 2 July 1830. Eighteen years later, eight years after the military had abolished his battalion, and only after being sentenced to death did he confess to his youthful flight from the rigours of military life. Clearly, Valerio preferred the freedom of a rogue.

Applying extant colonial and early national jurisprudence, the Federal Supreme Court rejected any claim Salto might have had to the *fuero militar*.[5] The Court noted that a defendant only had nine days after an ordinary jurisdiction judge initiated proceedings to claim the *fuero*. Legally, Salto had declined his rights to the *fuero* once he permitted a civilian court to hear the case against him and issue a sentence. Beyond that, constitutional law limited trials and appeals to three instances. After three instances, the law considered any sentence definitive and irrevocable.

The Supreme Court also rejected the military commandant's request for jurisdiction, citing a series of eighteenth-century royal orders and decrees that explicitly stated that a deserter who committed robbery or assault lost his right to the *fuero militar*.[6] Republican legislators had left no room for doubt on that point: a 13 February 1824 decree clearly stated

---

[4] According to decrees dated 2 September 1846 and 30 November 1846, enlisted men accused of military crimes were to be tried by a council of war composed of captains; for officers the council was composed of senior officers and presided over by the regional commander general; second and third instances were to be decided by the supreme military tribunal. If the sentence involved the death penalty, more than five years in a *presidio*, or expulsion from the army, the law required a mandatory sentencing review. See Mariano Galván Rivera, *Curia filípica mexicana* (México, 1850), pp. 136–42. As will be discussed, Salto quite clearly did not know all the applicable law concerning his status as a deserter.

[5] For applicable jurisprudence, see Juan N. Rodríguez de San Miguel, *Pandectas hispano-mexicanas, Estudio introductorio de María del Refugio González* (México, 1991), vol. II, pp. 1–142. Originally published in 1852, the 1991 facsimile edition includes royal orders, decrees, *cedulas*, and regulations along with national era laws and regulations; Rodríguez de San Miguel carefully noted national legislation that altered colonial jurisprudence.

[6] Casasola, *Colección de alegaciones y respuestas fiscales*. That jurisprudence included a 25 May 1773 royal order, a 6 May 1785 royal order, and royal decrees dated 9 February and 11 December 1793. See Rodríguez de San Miguel, *Pandectas* for those orders and decrees.

that any deserter arrested by civilian authorities on any criminal charge became immediately subject to ordinary jurisdiction courts and sentences. Valerio Salto could not evade civilian justice. Still, with the Supreme Court in transit from Querétaro to Mexico City in June 1848 and with a full docket through the summer, the Court did not reject the military commandant's claim until late September 1848.[7] Salto had won a delay.

Voluminous military justice records in the Mexican Supreme Court and in the Archivo General de la Nación reveal that neither Salto's crime nor his sentence was unusual. Desertion, robbery, assault, abduction, rape, and murder cases in military jurisdiction are amply documented.[8] Additionally, first instance and appellate military case files, correspondence and reports indicated a dangerous and violent public culture in early national Mexico. Reports from regional commandants offer even more indications of extraordinary levels of violence and extraordinary punishments.[9] The military, even though granted

---

[7] For the activities of the Supreme Court during the spring and summer of 1848, see, *Archivo de la Suprema Corte de Justicia de la Nación* (México), [Anexo], *Libro 7, Actas del Tribunal Pleno,* 2 August 1847–21 December 1848; hereafter, ASCJ.

[8] A cursory count of criminal cases that came before the national military appellate court between 1838 and 1854 yielded 354 desertion (absent from roll call for four days) cases, 512 desertion from guard duty cases, 84 jail breaks, 315 homicide cases, 250 physical injury cases, over 800 robbery cases with many of these cases involving more than one suspect. See Arnold, 'Inventario del antiguo Archivo del Tribunal de Guerra y Marina, 1816–1854', *Archivo de la Suprema Corte de Justicia [Anexo], Libro 589,* typescript transcription (1995), 397 pp. Scattered throughout what are chiefly military jurisdiction civil cases in the Archivo General de la Nación (México), Ramo de Civil (legajos) are first instance case files of abduction, rape, and statutory rape cases. See, for example, leg. 41, part 4b, 1847, D. José Mendosa acusando criminalmente al Subten. D. Francisco Fortenla por rapto; leg. 41, part 4b, 1851, Da. María Badillo de Monterrey contra el Sargento Pedro Ybarra y complices por rapto de su hija; leg. 41, part 4b, 1850, Prueba del Sr. Cor. Ventura Zamora [en la causa por seducción, estupro y rapto de la Sra. Da. María Barcenilla]; leg. 95, 1850, Criminal contra la Señora Da. Ana Gonzáles de Gonzáles por rapto de una niña menor; leg. 95, 1850, Criminal contra el Capt. D. José María Arenas por rapto de Da. Abundia Somoano; leg. 110, part 2B, 1836, D. José Antonio Araugo por D. Vicente Bassoco, toca a la sumaria instruída contra los autores del rapto de la Religiosa Manuela Bedía que sigue Féliz Osores del Provisorato Metropolitano; leg. 130, part 3A, 1840, Criminal contra el Comandante de Escuadron D. Miguel Rayon por el rapto de Da. María de Gaona [hija del Gral. D. Antonio Gaona]; and leg. 130, part 3A, 1822, Criminal sumaria contra el Ten. de Reg. de Cavallería número diez D. Ramon Puerta acusado del delito de violencia hecha con rapto, y estupro a Da. Ynocencia Montes de Oca; hereafter, AGN, Civil. See Arnold, 'Catálogo del Ramo de Civil', 4 MEG, 1992.

[9] For regional commander reports on prison visits, status of cases, and sentences, see Arnold, *Transcription;* and Arnold, *Inventario preliminar del Ramo Archivo de Guerra en el Archivo General de la Nación* (México, 1995), typescript, 96 pp. (Inventory of 1463 volume record set of national appellate military court archives and Commandancy General of Mexico judicial archives, 1810s–1860s.) This latter record set is difficult to consult: even though there are hundreds of volumes that contain case files, those files are bound together without any organising principle. One might find a military law case from 1843, a criminal case from 1829, and a military law case from 1852 bound together. Similarly, while volumes 450–3 contain 1849 reports on prisoners in military jurisdiction and military jails, those for 1843 are in volumes 1290, 1291, and 1293; those for the 1853–55 period can be found in volumes 548, 549, 555–7, 1028, 1099, 1357–67, and 1370–73; and those for 1822–26 are in volume 1276, which also contains pass-

jurisdiction over gangs and individuals who committed crimes throughout the rural countryside between March 1823 and the early 1830s, and again during the early 1840s and still again during the early 1850s, clearly could not simultaneously serve as rural police and guarantor of national security. Merely policing the military proved an overwhelming task.

Challenged by the reporting requirements, early national military bureaucrats performed no less ably as inveterate paper pushers than their colonial counterparts. Indeed, the volume and scope of case files and administrative records generated by the military judicial bureaucracy testify to the vibrancy of the military corporation in early national Mexico. Expanded and effectively bureaucratised during the late eighteenth century, the army after Independence inherited a dynamic judicial tradition. After Independence military bureaucrats prepared status reports on personnel and munitions; produced tables on prisoners, their crimes, the status of cases, and sentences; and conducted summary investigations of every officer who ever lost a battle, retreated in battle, or abandoned a position. That bureaucracy also adjudicated thousands of civil and criminal cases.

Some decades ago Lyle McAlister commented that the late colonial expansion of access to the military justice system contributed to the emergence of the army as 'an autonomous and irresponsible institution' after Independence. Concluding that members of the corporate military abused the *fuero militar*, McAlister argued that 'the administration of justice was hampered, public order disturbed, and royal authority weakened ... Nor did the end of Spanish dominion and the establishment of the republic solve the problem'.[10] Christon Archer explained: 'This was the first *fuero* open to almost anyone who could shoulder a musket, and it was only natural that elements to be found on the borderline of legality in any society would flaunt their privileges and use legal loopholes to escape pun-

---

ports issued by military authorities in Tampico, Querétaro, Saltillo, Monterrey, and Matamoros between 1840 and 1843 along with the May 1855 Plaza de México manpower report.

Compounding confusion, the Archivo de Guerra contains paperwork and case files from the judicial archives of the old Captaincy General, the Commandancy General of Mexico, and the Supreme Tribunal of War and Naval Affairs; and it includes cases involving individuals in the national/federal military and the nationally/federally activated militias. Still, the documentation is amazingly rich. For example, the documentation for the 1823 court martial of General José Antonio López de Santa Anna after he marched into San Luis Potosí and proclaimed a federal republic are in volumes 458 and 459. Records pertaining to the 1827 Padre Joaquín Arenas conspiracy can be found in volumes 439, 440, 501–3, 722, and 1377; and volume 726 includes the 1821–22 concubinage case initiated by the Bishop of Durango against Arenas. Volume 520 includes the summary court martial documents for the 1841 conspiracy case against Nicolás Bravo and Juan Alvarez, including the 'impresos en que se insulta a los generales Santa Anna y Tornel'. Conspiracy, murder, insubordination, assassination and robbery cases abound.

[10] Lyle N. McAlister, *The 'Fuero Militar' in New Spain, 1764–1800* (Westport, CN, 1957, 1974), pp. 15 and 88–89.

ishment.' Still, as Archer stressed, 'Generally speaking, Spanish military law and procedures carried impartial, if rigorous, justice'.[11]

More recently, historians have drawn on the historiography of the late colonial era to explain the persistence of the corporate military in early national Mexico. Reflecting that approach and conventional wisdom, David Bushnell and Neill Macaulay concurred with McAlister, commenting, 'The army would jealously guard its corporate privileges, or *fueros*, which exempted its personnel — including off-duty militia officers — from the jurisdictions of civilian courts in all matters, criminal and civil. The government in independent Mexico was not in a position to deprive the military of its privileges'.[12] Such conventional wisdom is based on research into the late colonial Bourbon military, not on research into the *fuero militar* after Independence; and in fact, the early national military judicial archives contain evidence that contradicts conventional wisdom. To wit, individuals entitled to the *fuero militar* did not wait for the government to curtail their 'privileges'. The law permitted individuals subject to military jurisdiction to subordinate themselves to ordinary jurisdiction courts. To do so, and in order to avoid possible reversals of judicial decisions based on technicalities, individuals filed *declinatoria de fuero* petitions with the military courts. Petitions filed with the Commandancy General of Mexico indicate that the several senior officers who held that post approved all those petitions.[13] Evidently, contrary to Bushnell and Macaulay's generalisation, senior military officers did not believe they needed to guard their corporation's prerogatives jealously.

The colonial legacy of a corporate military and a system of corporate military justice did persist in Mexico through the 1850s. During that early national era republican laws, decrees and regulations shaped the jurisdiction of the corporate military and its structure of justice. To insure national centralisation of that system, executive and legislative authorities agreed in January 1822 to create a national supreme council of war.[14]

---

[11] Christon I. Archer, *The Army in Bourbon Mexico, 1760–1810* (Albuquerque, 1977), pp. 16 and 275.

[12] David Bushnell and Neill Macaulay, *The Emergence of Latin America in the Nineteenth Century*, 2nd ed. (New York and Oxford, 1994), pp. 61–2.

[13] For a representative sampling of 'declinatoria de fuero' cases, see, AGN, Civil (legajos), leg. 6, part 2A, 1855, El Lic. D. Luis Ezeta declinando fuero; leg. 6, part 2A, 1854, D. José María Espinosa declinando fuero; leg. 38, 1838, D. Francisco Bustamante, declinatoria del fuero; leg. 38, 1839, El Sr. Gral. D. Manuel Barrera declinando fuero; leg. 48, part 2C, 1854, D. José Hoffman declinando fuero; leg. 57, part 2B, 1824, El Capt. D. Francisco González sobre declinatoria de fuero; leg. 76, 1849, El Ten. Cor. D. Ventura Zamora declinando jurisdicción; leg. 109, part 3A, 1846, Yncidente de declinatoria promovido por el Sr. Gral. D. Juan Nepomuceno Pérez en los autos [que sigue D. Manuel Yanguas Pérez]; leg. 110, part 2C, 1824, Ocurso echa por el Marqués de Salvatierra ... [toca a los réditos pertenecientes al Juzgado de Capellanías y declinatoria de fuero]; and leg. 130, part 1, 1836, El Capt. D. José María Barrera declinando jurisdicción de la demanda que le ha puesto ante el Sr. Juez de Letras D. Manuel Zozaya [D. Pedro Yturria, apoderado del Tercer Orden de San Francisco, contra Barrera sobre pesos].

[14] That council initiated its proceedings on 1 March 1822. See *Memoria presentada al So-*

Modelling that council on the supreme council authorised by the *cortes* for the Spanish empire, Mexican civilian and military politicians modified and specified the scope, authority, jurisdiction and responsibility along with the structures and functions of the military judicial bureaucracy in a March 1823 set of regulations.[15] Juridically, the seven senior officers who sat on the national appellate military court adjudicated military law cases; and they convened with Supreme Court magistrates to hear civil cases. In fact, under March 1823 and 23 May 1837 regulations, while military officers decided cases involving military law, only civilian judges convening with military judges could decide cases involving civil matters. At the appellate level, the senior officers on the national military appellate court had to meet with Supreme Court magistrates to review all lower military court capital punishment sentences; and together they would hear procedural appeals from lower military courts and review pardon requests, principally from those who had received capital punishment sentences.[16]

The May 1837 provisional judicial administration law made explicit and nationally applicable some jurisprudential innovations. First, it required all judges to cite jurisprudence rather than simply state findings.[17] Second, it required a mandatory sentencing review of all criminal sentences, whether the convicted party wanted a review or not. Third, it forbade the courts from prohibiting the publication of briefs, case files, or any documents pertaining to any case, except of course confidential or secret information. That opened the judicial process to public view and reinvigorated the legal publications industry in Mexico.[18] Finally, the provisional

---

berano Congreso Mexicano por el Secretario de Estado y del Despacho de la Guerra (México, 1822; and AGN, Ramo del Real Acuerdo, vol. 11, 1 March 1822.

[15] *Reglamento provisional para las funciones y servicio del Estado Mayor General de los ejércitos de la república mexicana, y estados y noticias que deben dar los cuerpos y secciones divisionarias* (México, 1823). For the structure of the military judicial bureaucracy, see Tables 1 and 2.

[16] Because military judges convened with Supreme Court magistrates, the Archivo de la Suprema Corte de la Nación [Anexo] still conserves a number of military court records, including proceedings of plenum and chamber sessions. See, for example, ASCJ, [Anexo], Libros 609–11, 'Numeración de Autoridades (Tribunal de Guerra), 1857–1860'; and Libro 1259, 'Cuaderno de entradas de los negocios de la Primera Sala de la Corte Marcial, 1837–1842'. The majority of the extant documentation from the archive of the military court is located in AGN, Archivo de Guerra; the Ramo de Suprema Corte also contains ample military jurisdiction documentation. See, for example, pardon reviews in AGN, Ramo de Suprema Corte, caja 18, leg. 3 (1840); caja 19, leg. 1 (1840); leg. 4 (1840); caja 20, leg. 5 (1840); and caja 31, leg. 3 (1841).

[17] See Basilio Arrillaga, *Recopilación de leyes, decretos, bandos, reglamentos, circulares y providencia de los supremos poderes y otras autoridades de la república mexicana . . . 1837* (México, 1839), 'Arreglo provisional de la administración de justicia en los tribunales y juzgados del fuero común', 23 May 1837; and 'Reglamento para el gobierno interior de la Suprema Corte Marcial, formada por ella misma', 6 September 1837. Innumerable case files indicate that judges began to cite jurisprudence when that law went into effect.

[18] Jaime del Arenal Fenochio, 'Ojeada a la historiografía sobre las instituciones jurídicas del siglo XIX', in María del Refugio González (comp.), *Historia del derecho* (México, 1992), pp. 154–80. Del Arenal noted that recently Universidad Nacional Autónoma de México has sponsored the publication in facsimile of many of the basic nineteenth-century works otherwise

regulation explicitly required all courts and tribunals in the discovery, substantiation, and judicial decision-making stages to cite and apply established jurisprudence in all civil and criminal cases; subsequently, courts and tribunals complied with that requirement.

The 1837 innovations applied equally to constitutional, ordinary, and military jurisdiction courts, even though some preferred less law and more order. Indeed, those committed to a liberal state and a secularised society acted collectively to transform social institutions and to limit the militarisation of the criminal justice system. Unlike the regional commandant in Michoacán during the late 1840s, even some high level military officers actively participated in that process. For example, having received a copy of a 5 October 1839 executive order to try thieves and murderers in military courts, General José Joaquín de Herrera, then the regional commandant general in Puebla, sent the Supreme Court a copy of the order and expressed his concern about the militarisation of criminal justice. Responding, the Supreme Court asked Defence Secretary Juan Nepomuceno Almonte to explain why he had issued the order. After all, the Supreme Court magistrates believed it was a Mexican national's constitutional right to be tried in a jurisdictionally competent court. Almonte brusquely justified the expansion of the military jurisdiction, stating that the purpose of the order was '... to save society, which is threatened by imminent ruin'.[19] Most assuredly unconvinced that broadening the jurisdiction of military courts would save civil society, the Supreme Court submitted the issue to the Supremo Poder Conservador, requesting that 'moderating power' declare Almonte's decree unconstitutional.

Reacting to the persistence of the culture of violence after Independence, early national legislators in September 1823 approved a law authorising the military to arrest and try bandits, rogues and other dangerous people. Civilian politicians continued to permit the militarisation of criminal justice until the Federal Congress on December 1832 rescinded that law. The 1832 law ordered the immediate transfer of all ordinary jurisdiction criminal cases to first instance civilian courts and ordered military and militia troops in the future to transfer suspects to the proper civilian authorities within 48 hours of their arrest.[20] When Almonte's 1839 decree

---

difficult to locate and consult. For a comprehensive review and bibliography of colonial legal publications, see Sergei Alexander Mayagoitia Stone, 'Notas para servir a la bibliografía jurídica novohispana: la literatura circunstancial', 2 vols. (Tésis para obtener el título de Licenciado en Derecho: Facultad de Derecho, Universidad Nacional Autónoma de México, 1992).

[19] AGN, Suprema Corte, caja 17, 1839, leg. 10, arch. 389 (Expediente 95), 'Expediente sobre que se excite al Supremo Poder Conservador para que declare nula la orden del Supremo Gobierno de 5 de octubre del presente año por la que autorizó a los comandantes generales para juzgar a los ladrones y asesinos'.

[20] See Arrillaga, *Recopilación ... 1832*, 18 December 1832, 'Ley. Cesan las leyes que expresa relativas a ladrones, y otros reos que deben ser juzgados militarmente'; and ASCJ, Libro 1043-2, 'secretaría de la primera sala ... Causas remitidas por la Comandancia General por

and the Supreme Court objection to it reached the Supremo Poder Conservador, its members agreed with the Supreme Court that the defence secretary lacked the authority to create new law. Accordingly, the 'moderating power' declared the decree unconstitutional on 25 January 1840. While that did not stop some national leaders from further efforts to militarise criminal justice, it did reinforce the political value of the supremacy of civil society and the value of a constitutionally limited national executive authority. Nevertheless, Almonte's concerns were not without foundation.

Criminal trial and military prison records only begin to shed light on the early national culture of violence. Complementing those records are the *partes de novedades* reports, dating from the 1820s through the 1840s. Through those reports local military officers, assigned to duty stations throughout the state/department of Mexico, kept the Commandancy General of Mexico informed about local rumblings of discontent.[21] Even though any number of those reports simply state '*no hay novedades*', in their totality they offer glimpses into stresses and responses throughout the most populous state in Mexico. When studied in tandem with sedition, conspiracy, rebellion, and political cases, the *partes de novedades* offer historians the opportunity to track forms and levels of discontent among ordinary people in Mexico's most populous region during the early national republic.

Even in the face of what all recognised as a dangerous environment, many individuals maintained their faith in pursuing advantage through the courts, as evidenced by the countless civil cases in military jurisdiction. And even though rather mundane debt cases make up the majority of civil law cases, there are also child custody cases, child and wife support cases, a fair number of salary garnishing cases, and the occasional suit against the military paymaster.[22] For example, when Squadron Commander D. Do-

---

no seguir conociendo en ella, por haverse derogada la ley de 27 de setiembre de 1823. Distribuídas a los Jueces de Letras'.

[21] Torcuato S. di Tella several decades ago urged historians ' ... to realise that there were various sorts of masses to be mobilised, according to the stresses they were undergoing'. The *partes de novedades* offer historians raw information about those stresses and the varying and various responses of ordinary folk throughout central Mexico. See his 'The Dangerous Classes in Early Nineteenth Century Mexico', *Journal of Latin American Studies*, vol. 5, no. 1, p. 81. For the *partes de novedades* reports, see AGN, Archivo de Guerra. *Partes de novedades* are interspersed throughout innumerable volumes in this record set. See, for example, vol. 789, 1834–38; vol. 925, 1834; vol 951, 1836–37; vol. 1089, 1840–41; vol. 1812, 1839; and vol. 1276, 1825. Impressionistically, the documentation for 1838 and 1839 may be the most comprehensive.

[22] Most civil cases concluded at the first instance level. Those cases for the Commandancy General of Mexico are located in AGN, Civil (legajos). That record set is composed of two documentary groupings. The documents in the bound volumes primarily are the archived cases and documents from the civil chamber of the colonial *audiencia* and the viceregal *escribanía de gobierno y guerra*; the unbound bundles are a tremendous judicial notarial archive that includes civil cases from Mexico City ordinary jurisdiction courts, and civil cases in military jurisdiction. The cases date from the early eighteenth century into the 1860s, permitting an evaluation of continuity and change particularly in civil case adjudication, as well as any number of other topics due to the vastness of the documentation.

mingo Soto Mayor received orders to proceed to Durango as part of Mexico's post-US/Mexican war effort to contain the *indios bárbaros* in the north, he left his wife, Da. Porfiria Gaytán, in Mexico City. Finding herself without financial resources, Da. Porfiria filed a suit in military court to force the military paymaster to direct one third of her husband's salary to Mexico City rather than all of it to Durango.[23] The military court upheld the impoverished spouse's suit, ordering the Durango paymaster to forward one third of the Soto Mayor's salary to Mexico City. In this particular instance, the officer supported his wife's suit. In other instances, the courts had to force military men to assume their responsibilities. Fathers did receive court orders to support their 'natural' children.[24] And in the case of garnished salaries, the courts ordered paymasters to deduct one third of an individual's salary until debts were redeemed.[25] Of the two dozen or so garnished salary cases, most date from the late 1840s and early 1850s, probably because earlier members of the military had difficulty getting paid, making judicial orders moot.

Reflective of the financial difficulties of military officers, and calling into question the conventional wisdom that a military/ecclesiastical corporate alliance emerged to strengthen both corporations during the early national era, is documentation on several hundred non-payment of rent and vacate premises cases. While individual property owners filed suits against military personnel for non-payment of rent, such as the suit Da. Ysabel Rendón filed against General Manuel María Lombardini in 1842, many of the plaintiffs in those cases were ecclesiastical organisations.[26] Ecclesiastical

---

[23] AGN, Civil (legajos), leg. 23, part 2b, 1850, Da. Porfiria Gaytán, sobre que su esposo el Comandante de Escuadrón D. Domingo Soto Mayor le dé alimentos. There are about two dozen first instance military jurisdiction *'sobre alimentos'* cases: see for example, see leg. 33, part 2a, 1853, Da. Teresa García contra D. Tomás Prieto por alimentos; leg. 48, part 2c, 1854, Da. Francisca Hernandes contra el Sr. Cor. D. José Torres Valdibia sobre alimentos; and leg. 97, 1828, Da. María del Carmen Bersunsa contra su marido el Ten. Cor. D. Eduardo Rodríguez sobre alimentos.

[24] AGN, Civil (legajos), leg. 225, part 3, 1836, Da. María Ygnacia Llanos de Vergara con el Capt. D. Victoriano Roa [de Bergara] sobre que le ministre alimentos a una hija natural; leg. 226, part 1, 1854, D. Julián Carrión pide que el Capt. D. Manuel Gerardino dé alimentos a sus hijos naturales. For other examples of cases involving natural children, see leg. 45, part 4, 1826, Quaderno corriente de los autos promovidos por Da. Vibiana Peres de Tagle contra D. José María Beltrán [sobre la herencia de la hija natural de D. Severo Beltrán, padre de la segunda parte]; leg. 45, part 4, 1835, Guadalupe Basques contra Capt. Nestor Relles por un hijo natural; leg. 163, part 2, 1824, Da. Rafaela Morenza, contra el Sr. Cor. D. José María Travesi sobre alimentos; and leg. 225, part 5, 1830, El soldado Cristoval Ruiz con José Luque, sobre entrega de una hija natural.

[25] See, for example, AGN, Civil (legajos) leg. 6, part 2a, 1853, Cesión de la tercera parte de su sueldo para pago de sus acredores que hace el Comandante de Escuadrón D. Jesús Escudero; leg. 18, part 3b, 1843, el Sr. Cor. D. Joaquín Gómez Luna sobre que se le descuente la tercera parte de su sueldo para pago del crédito que expresa; and leg. 23, part 2b, 1851, El Capt. D. Miguel Guardia haciendo cesión de su sueldo para pago de sus acreedores.

[26] AGN, Civil (legajos), leg. 48, part 3c, 1842, Da. Ysabel Rendón con el Sr. Gral. D. Manuel María Lombardini sobre pesos [arrendamientos] y desocupación de casa. Most assuredly not

plaintiffs, as with all plaintiffs, had to sue a defendant in the defendant's jurisdiction; consequently, in spite of conflict of jurisdiction briefs filed by the legal counsels of ecclesiastical organisations, suits against military defendants for unpaid rent had to be filed in the military courts. Mexican jurisprudence also required that plaintiffs and defendants submit to arbitration before incurring the expense of a court case.[27] Still, many cases went to court. While those cases reflect the extensive economic power of the corporate church, one might wonder just how much power the church wielded when it had to sue to collect rent. And even a partial list of ecclesiastical plaintiffs indicates that getting tenants to pay rent presented a challenge for numerous ecclesiastical organisations. Those plaintiffs included the Convento de San Camilo, the Convento de Santo Domingo, the Convento de Santa Catarina, the Convento de N. S. de la Encarnación, the Convento de San Juan de la Penitencia, the Colegio de San Angel de Carmelitas Descalzos, the Convento de Regina, the Convento de San José de Gracia, and the Colegio de San Gregorio, to name just a few landlords.[28] As many of the case files indicated, urban renters, military officers, and their widows were not trying to take advantage of the church; rather, from the late 1830s and into the 1850s they simply did not have the cash to pay rent.

Not all who had the right to have cases heard in military jurisdiction lacked substantial cash, as illustrated by the vast documentation on textile impresario and 'general' Manuel Barrera.[29] Among the dozen or so cases and

---

intimidated by a high ranking military officer, Sr. Laisne de Villeveque sued Cor. Joaquín Ayestaran for back rent in 1838, see leg. 154, part 1b, 1838, El Sr. Laisne de Villeveque demandando al Sr. Cor. D. Joaquín de Ayestaran, Ayudante General de la Plaza Mayor, la cantidad de doscientos veinte pesos de arrendamiento de casa.

[27] For arbitration documentation, see AGN, Civil (legajos) leg, 226, part 1, varios (Juicios verbales de varios años seguídos en el fuero de guerra sobre demanda de varios conventos por desocupación de casa y renta). See also, for example, leg. 4, 1830s, Carpeta de juicios verbales; leg. 18, part 3b, 1839, Cuaderno de pruebas de los juicios verbales; leg. 23, part 1, 1853, Libro de juicios verbales (enero–marzo); and leg. 159, part 2, 1847–54, Juicios verbales, citas y conciliaciones habidas de 1847 hasta 1854 (29 cuadernos).

[28] Just to cite a few examples, see AGN, Civil (legajos), leg. 4, 1837, La parte del Tercer Orden contra Sr. Cor. D. Nicomedes del Callejo sobre pago de renta; leg. 28, 1837 [La parte del Convento de Santa Catalina de Sena contra la testamentaria del Gral. D. Pedro Zarzosa sobre pesos [arrendamiento]; leg. 48, 3b, 1853, D. Manuel María Melgarejo por el R. P. Procurador del Convento de Santo Domingo contra D. Manuel Saviñón por pesos y desocupación de casa; and leg. 73, 1839, D. Agustín Elguea en representación del Convento de la Encarnación, con la viuda Sra. Da. María Rodríguez de Tafor sobre arrendamientos de casa.

[29] For case files and other legal manoeuvering, see, AGN, Civil, (legajos), leg. 38, 1839, el Sr. Gral. D. Manuel Barrera, declinando fuero; leg. 97, 1848, la testamentaria del Sr. Gral. D. Manuel Barrera contra D. Luis Abila; leg. 119, 1835, Contra el Sr. Gral. D. Manuel Barrera por haber dado golpes a el Lic. D. José María Múñoz de Cote; leg. 130, 1826, Cor. D. Manuel Barrera contra Cor. Graduado D. José Gómez Aguado sobre pesos; leg. 133, 1836, Denuncia hecho por el Sr. Gral. D. Manuel Barrera [por 'atroces injurias'] de un artículo inserto en el periódico *Mosquito*, del día cinco de julio de 1836; leg. 133, 1836, [Que el Sr. Gral. D. Manuel Barrera se presentase en la garita a extraer cantidad de pesos; leg. 200, part 2, 1850, Germán Durantón como cesionario de los herederos del Sr. Gral. D. Manuel Barrera contra

documents involving Barrera are Sra. María Ignacia Rodríguez de Velasco's 1826 suit against Barrera, in which she alleged that he unlawfully confiscated her balcony seat at the bullfights. The following decade Lic. José María Múñoz de Cote pursued criminal assault charges against Barrera after Múñoz de Cote verbally confronted the 'general', who in reaction to confrontation allegedly struck Múñoz de Cote. With extenuating circumstances, Barrera got off; Lic. Múñoz de Cote went on to become a successful judge.

The value of Barrera's personal wealth and estate were recorded in several cases. The impresario personally contracted the French caterer M. Zephire Dupuin and financed four lavish banquets in Tlalpan for General José Antonio López de Santa Anna when he returned to the executive in late 1841. After the four *comidas* in December 1841, Dupuin submitted a 781 peso bill that included lost or 'stolen' items. According to a list of missing items Dupuin submitted with his bill, a few of the guests apparently took silver spoons, copper serving trays, cooking utensils, and napkins as souvenirs of the occasion, or just simply stole Dupuin's property, leading one to wonder about some of the company Barrera and Santa Anna kept. Evidently, Barrera neglected or refused to pay Dupuin, who filed suit and, as required, entered arbitration in June 1842. Municipal judge Mariano Riva Palacio found in Dupuin's favour; however, three months later Barrera still had not paid his debt, much less Dupuin's court costs. Dupuin, facing financial hardship and commercial bankruptcy, filed suit in the military court. Suggestive of just how much gumption it took to sue a wealthy and powerful man, Dupuin commented in his September statement, 'Que muy perjudicial es litigar contra personas grandes...'. Boldness may have served Dupuin. With no additional evidence of legal problems between the general and the caterer, apparently Barrera responded differently to orders from the military court than he had to orders from Riva Palacio, a noted and unabashed political liberal of the era.

Seemingly, paying Dupuin would not threaten the textile impresarios's financial wellbeing. Following his death in 1845, his widow provided a comprehensive inventory of his estate. With a collection of precious gems and jewels valued at over 21,000 pesos, shares in a Fresnillo silver mine, houses in Tlalpan, Coyoacán, Panzacola, and Mexico City, interests in cockfighting and bullfighting, and a maguey field and textile factory in Panzacola, Barrera had become one of the wealthiest men in Mexico at the time of his death. Nevertheless, living in a risky credit economy, Barrera had also ac-

---

el exmo Sr. Gral. D. José María Tornel; leg. 200, part 2, 1850, Prueba promovida por el Sr. Gral. D. José María Tornel en los autos que sigue con D. Germán Durantón sobre pesos; leg. 200, part 2, 1846, Yncidente en los autos seguídos por D. Angel Trebilla en representación de la casa de Sr. Agüero contra la testamentaria del Sr. Gral. D. Manuel Barrera; leg 200, part 4, 1840, D. German Duranton como cesionario de D. Manuel Barrera y Prieto contra el Sr. Capt. D. Marcelo Alvarez, sobre pesos; leg. 200, part 4, 1842, M. Zephire Dupuin contra el Sr. Gral D. Manuel Barrera, sobre pesos; and leg. 208, 1826, [Sra. Da. María Ygnacia Rodríguez de Velasco contra Sr. Cor. D. Manuel de la Barrera].

cumulated significant debts that neared or exceeded the value of his estate.[30] And the size of Barrera's estate was exceptional. Most members of the military, as most ordinary folk, died without much, if any, property. In fact, by the early 1840s the military judicial notary in Mexico City had begun to file suits against estates for nonpayment of recording fees.[31]

Barrera's court experiences aside, most commonly, civil suits in military jurisdiction involved small, simple debts, even though some unusual and gossipy cases remain in the archival record.[32] Among the more gossipy cases, Agata Serafina Cheret of Paris filed a suit against the powerful military politician General José Ignacio de Basadre, who apparently hadn't paid his rent when he was in Paris in 1834. After her husband had died, Cheret pursued the debt in Mexico.[33]

And lest one think military officers lacked high culture, Sra. Dolores Cordero had to file two suits in military court before she could get her piano returned to her. She had signed a contract with Col. Sebastián Moro del Moral in May 1850, obliging the colonel to pay a monthly rental fee for the use of her piano.[34] Six months later, after the colonel had neglected to pay even a single month's rent, Cordero sued him for nonpayment. During that suit, Cordero learned that Moro del Moral had sold her piano to pay a 240 peso debt his son owed to General Juan Manuel Lasquelty. Even though she won her suit against Mora del Moral, Cordero had to file a second law suit to recover her property from Lic. Félix Pavia, who held Lasquelty's power of attorney and control over his property because the general had left the country. The following March the military court ordered Pavia to return Cordero's piano to her and ordered the military paymaster to garnish one third of Moro del Moral's salary to pay his son's 240 peso debt with Lasquelty.

Did the military, as Bushnell and Macaulay stated, jealously guard its jurisdiction? Was the army an irresponsible institution, as McAlister commented? Were we to look only at the political machinations of a handful of high level military politicians, perhaps the response would be yes. And were we to limit the evidence to Valerio Salto's successfully manipulating his attorney and the regional military commandant in Michoacán in 1848 to delay the execution of his sentence, perhaps the response would be yes.

---

[30] AGN, Civil (legajos), leg., 5, 1845, La Sra. Da. Aleja Delgado de Barrera viuda y alvacea del Sr. Gral. D. Manuel Barrera solicitando licencia para la facción de ynventario por memorias extrajudiciales.

[31] AGN, Civil (legajos), leg. 38, 1842, [La escribanía de guerra contra varias testamentarias sobre derechos].

[32] Valuable for their rarity are the 1830s and 1840s accounting books for the hacienda of Santa Ysabla. See AGN, Civil (legajos) leg. 189, part 4, 1837, [Concurso de Esteban González de Cosio].

[33] AGN, Civil (legajos), leg. 200, part 4, 1834–51, D. Germán Durantón como apdo. jurídico de la Sra. Da. Agata Serafina Cheret viuda de D. Juan Enrique Hahn contra el Sr. Gral. D. José Ignacio de Basadre sobre pesos.

[34] AGN, Civil, leg. 274, 1850, La Sra. Da. Dolores Cordero contra el Sr. Cor. D. Sevastián Moro del Moral sobre devolución de un piano; for the only other reference to a piano see leg. 193, part 4, 1859, D. Feliciano P. Contreras contra D. Agustín Bernard sobre pesos [venta de un piano].

However, the distribution of conflict of jurisdiction cases suggests that authorities other than military commandants, notably local alcaldes and federal district and circuit judges, were vying for power during the first federal republic. More importantly, though, military, constitutional and ordinary jurisdiction case files reveal that judges applied jurisprudence not corporate biases when they decided guilt or innocence, determined liability, and issued definitive sentences.

That those entitled to the *fuero militar* might have hoped to get preferential treatment from their courts is understandable; after all, plaintiffs and even some defendants went to court to seek advantage. Creditors sued; lenders sued; even ecclesiastical authorities had little patience with those who didn't pay their rent. Prisoners appealed convictions and sentences; and the condemned actively sought pardons. Military judicial notaries compiled bundles and bundles of civil case files; and military bureaucrats produced thousands of reports on important as well as irrelevant minutia. There is no evidence to suggest that *justice* was any more or any less privileged in the military corporation than in ordinary jurisdiction. The *fuero militar* did not persist in Mexico simply because eighteenth century reformers initiated, and some elite political leaders believed in preserving, a tradition. No, the *fuero militar* persisted because thousands of people — plaintiffs, outlaws, abandoned wives and abandoned children, privates and corporals, attorneys and judges, guards and officers — actively asserted agency, albeit some not voluntarily, in corporate society. And some of those active participants in corporate society believed they would lose advantage were they cast adrift in the amorphous and violent public culture that the military tried so hard, yet failed, to contain throughout the early national era.

Appendix 1. The Bureaucracy of Military Justice

Supremo Tribunal de Guerra y Marina, 1823–37, 1846–53, 1860–63

Tribunal Pleno
    1a. Sala
        1a. Secretaría
    2a. Sala

    Fiscalía

Suprema Corte Marcial, 1837–46, 1853–55, 1858–60, 1863–67

Tribunal Pleno
    Sala De Ordenanza
    1a. Sala
        1a. Secretaría
    2a. Sala
        2a. Secretaría
    3a. Sala
        3a. Secretaría

    Fiscalía

Capitanía General de México (1535–1823)
Escribanía Mayor de Guerra

Estado Mayor (1823–28) y Comandancia General de México
Secretaría General: Sección Central

    Mesa 1a. Secretaría General
        Ordenes de Marcha, Movimientos de Militares Pases y
        Pasaportes,
        Correspondencia con el Ministerio de Guerra y Marina,
        Circulación de Leyes y Decretos, Negocios Reservados

    Mesa 2a. Secretaría de Administración
        Estados de Fuerza, Armas, Municiones, Vestuario y Montura;
        Pedidos de Armas, etc.; Correspondencia Relativa a las Revistas
        de los Cuerpos; Reclamaciones (Solicitudes); Retiros e Inválidos;
        Gastos (subsecuentamente: Mesa 4a.)
    Mesa 3a. Secretaría de Policía y Justicia

Desertores, Prisioneros, Causas Simples, Licencias Temporales, Remplazos, Hospitales Causas Criminales (Pliegos y Extractos de Causas)

Mesa 4a. Secretaría de Topografía y Estadística

Mesa 5a. Juzgado de Ladrones

Mesa 6a.

Plana Mayor

Comisaría General de Guerra y Marina

Appendix 2. Regional Command Centres

Comandancia General de México

Secretaría: Sección Divisionaria
Escribanía de Guerra
Plaza Mayor de La Ciudad de México
Sargentía Mayor
Comandancias Principales (Plazas)
Puntos Militares
Cárceles Militares
  Ex-Acordada
  Ex-Inquisición
  Huichiapán
  Naranjos
  Santiago Tlatelolco
Cantón de Jalapa
Cantón de Tacubaya
Comandancia General de Aguascalientes
Comandancia General de Baja California
Comandancia General de Chihuahua
Comandancia General de Chiapas
Comandancia General de Coahuila-Tejas
Comandancia General de Distrito Federal
Comandancia General de Durango
Comandancia General de Guanajuato
Comandancia General de Jalisco

Comandancia Principal de Colima
Comandancia General de Michoacán
Comandancia General de Nuevo León
Comandancia General de Oaxaca
Comandancia General de Puebla
Comandancia Principal de Tlaxcala
Comandancia General de Querétaro
Comandancia General de San Luis Potosí
Comandancia General de Sinaloa
Comandancia General de Sonora
Comandancia General de Tabasco
Comandancia General de Tamaulipas
Comandancia General de Tejas
Comandancia General de Veracruz
Comandancia General de Yucatán
Comandancia General de Zacatecas

División de Operaciones en Yucatán
Departamento de Marina del Norte
Dirección General de Artillería
Dirección General de Ingenieros

Source: Reglamento provisional para las funciones y servicio del Estado Mayor General de los ejércitos de la república mexicana, y estados y noticias que deben dar los cuerpos y secciones divisionarias (México, 1823).

CHAPTER 4

From Justice of the Peace to Social War in Rio de Janeiro, 1824–1841

Thomas H. Holloway

This chapter traces the development of the local level judicial system as an important feature in the formation of the Brazilian state. It might be said to begin with the transfer of Portuguese organisational patterns with the arrival of the Royal Court in 1808 with the subsequent maturation of national institutions toward the middle of the nineteenth century. It focuses on the legal principles underlying judicial authority over minor public order offences and criminal activity, with particular attention to the experiment with the institution of the justice of the peace in the 1820s and 1830s. The stage on which this process played out was primarily the city of Rio de Janeiro, the seat of the government and the setting of several institutional experiments in the realm of policing and judicial practice. The locally elected justice of the peace (JP) — proposed in the 1824 constitution, legally regulated in 1827, incorporated into the appointed judicial hierarchy during the early 1830s and relegated to a marginal and vestigial role by the judicial reform of December 1841 — was an anomaly in the judicial history of Brazil. The elected JP deviated in principle from the top down judicial system that preceded it, coexisted with it, and superseded it after a few short years of tentative experimentation.

An examination of the ideas behind the justice of the peace, how these local judges operated in practice, and the effective end of the experiment in locally elected magistrates, reveals much about the relationship between the emerging Brazilian state, the polity relevant to it and society more broadly. A general problem following formal Independence was how to replace the institutions by which the colony functioned in the interests of the colonial metropolis and the Portuguese commercial elite, with mechanisms by which the new state would operate in the interest of the Brazilian commercial elite and their essential partners engaged in export agriculture and extractive activities. The pragmatic leaders of post-colonial Brazil soon concluded that what they perceived as a kind of social war — the problem of maintaining control over the urban slave population and the free 'rabble' in the capital of the Brazilian Empire — necessitated a centralised hierarchy in which judicial authority was delegated from the minister of justice of the Empire down to the streets, alleys and waterfront of the national capital.

Among the principal areas of pressure for a clear break with the colonial past during the first decades of independence were the basic attributes of the state the Brazilians hoped to create: criminal legislation, judicial institutions and procedures, and the exercise of police power. In a broad sense, Brazil belatedly participated in the reform movement that swept the Atlantic world in the age of Enlightenment and revolution in the last half of the eighteenth century and first half of the nineteenth, a movement generally identified with liberal ideology. Brazilian liberals, and even conservative nationalists of the Independence period, saw the extant judicial institutions and procedures both as antiquated relics of a bygone era and as a legacy of colonial oppression. A dilemma emerged that reflected the contradictions of a liberal ideology within a highly stratified society held together by political patronage, economic exploitation and physical coercion. The political leaders wanted to move out from under colonial despotism and monarchical absolutism, while at the same time they recognised that any fundamental break in the relations of domination on which Brazil's society and economy rested could be dangerously disruptive to their own status and control.[1] In this context a locally elected lower judiciary seemed to be an appropriate innovation, but it soon succumbed to the socio-political realities of the era.

The Colonial Legacy

Brazilian judicial institutions during the colonial age had been established under the Afonsine code of the mid-fifteenth century, the Manueline Code of the early sixteenth century and the Philipine Code of the early seventeenth century. These compilations were themselves attempts to bring some order to the accretion over centuries of laws, decrees, customary practices and precedents which had their origins in ancient Rome and the Visigothic kingdoms that followed Roman rule in Iberia, as well as in the judicial practices of the Iberian inquisition.[2] In addition, there was a significant, but largely unacknowledged, influence from the judicial practices of the Moslem polities of medieval Iberia, seen lingering in such linguistic reminders as *alcaíde* (constable), *almotacél* (petty judge), *aljube* (ecclesiastical jail), and *meirinho* (bailiff).

As Brazil became increasingly important in the eighteenth century as the economic lifeblood of Portugal, a series of reforms inspired by European enlightened despotism made colonial control more pervasive and efficient from the Portuguese perspective, and more oppressive to the emerging group of Brazilian nativists. Portugal established an elaborate

---

[1] An informed and insightful collection of essays, in which the contradictions of Brazilian liberalism is a recurring theme, is Emília Viotti da Costa, *The Brazilian Empire, Myths and Histories* (Chicago, 1985), esp. pp. 53–77.

[2] Stuart Schwartz, *Sovereignty and Society in Colonial Bahia: The High Court of Bahia and its Judges, 1609–1751* (Berkeley, 1973), pp. 45–54; Candido Mêndes de Almeida (ed.), *Código philippino; ou, ordenaçôes e leis do reino de Portugal ... décima quarta ediçâo segundo a primeira de 1603 e a nona de Coimbra de 1824 ...* . (Rio de Janeiro, 1870).

judicial system in its colonies which was essential to the maintenance of the empire, and judges were among the principal representatives of the monarchical authority and colonial control Brazilians grew to resent. Criminal law was governed by Book V of the Philipine Code, which specified the mechanisms of absolutism. Only agents of the crown, and not private individuals, could initiate proceedings. Only royal judges could collect and evaluate evidence, deciding what was relevant and what was to be excluded, and judicial torture was an important instrument for extracting confessions. Trials pitted the judge together with the prosecutor against the defendant, who had no rights; proceedings could be held in secret if the judge saw fit. And legal punishments included physical mutilation, branding, drawing and quartering and whipping.[3]

The police intendancy

In Rio de Janeiro the local-level judiciary system changed before formal Independence, as the transferral of the Portuguese Court to Brazil brought the establishment of the General Intendant of Police of the Court and the State of Brazil on 10 May 1808. This police intendancy was based on the French model, first established in Portugal in 1760, with responsibility for public works and ensuring the provisioning of the city, in addition to personal and collective security.[4] These responsibilities included public order, surveillance of the population, the investigation of crimes, and apprehension of criminals. Like the judges of Rio's high court of appeals, the intendant held the rank of *desembargador*, and he was also considered a minister of state. He had the power to decide what behaviour was to be declared criminal, establish the punishment he thought appropriate, and then to arrest, prosecute, pass judgement, and supervise the sentence of individual perpetrators. He thus represented the authority of the absolute monarch, and consistent with colonial administrative practice the office combined legislative, executive (police), and judicial powers. The royal decree establishing the intendancy confirmed the concept of granting judicial authority over minor offences to the police, in the following terms:

> As there are crimes that require no punishment other than some correction, the Intendant may in such cases arrest such persons as deserve correction, keeping them imprisoned for a time judged by the Intendant as proportional to the disorder committed, and as seems necessary for correction.[5]

---

[3] Astolpho Rezende, 'Polícia administrativa, polícia judiciária, o código do processo de 1832, a lei de 3 de dezembro de 1841, a lei de 20 de setembro de 1871', Instituto Histórico e Geográfico Brasileiro, *Primeiro Congresso de História Nacional*, 4 vols. (Rio de Janeiro, 1916), vol. 3, p. 402.

[4] Elysio de Araujo, *Estudo histórico sobre a polícia da capital federal* (Rio de Janeiro, 1898), pp. 10–27.

[5] Quoted in Aurelino Leal, 'História judiciária do Brasil', in *Diccionário histórico*

In order to assist the intendant in those aspects of his varied responsibility relating to 'correcting' unacceptable behaviour, on 27 June 1808 the prince regent divided the city into two judicial districts and established the new position of criminal judge (*juiz do crime*) for each. The criminal judges were subordinate to the intendant, and had the same combination of judicial and police functions in their districts as he had over the city as a whole.[6] This institutional structure remained in place in Rio de Janeiro through the subsequent political stages culminating in Independence in September 1822, and on into the first empire, as the reign of Pedro I is known.

The Justice of the Peace

The locally elected lay judge was a project envisioned in the 1824 Constitution and dear to the hearts of the liberal reformers of the early years of Independence. As the first clear break with the concept of judicial authority emanating from the monarch, the justice of the peace had the potential to be a major turning point in the way power was exercised and society regulated.[7] The proposal for instituting the justice of the peace was debated from 1823 onwards, and the law authorising the institution was approved in 1827. From the start, the main proponents of the institution saw the police function of the local judge as central to their purpose. Bernardo Pereira de Vasconcellos, a central figure in the liberal reform group and an advocate of the new judicial position, said in parliament in June 1827 that 'we want to establish a magistrate that I will call "of police" (*policial*). Even though the name does not strike me as very appropriate, I will leave it at that'. Vasconcellos went on to criticise the traditional approach to policing in Brazil, which focused on punishment after a crime was committed. The justice of the peace, he said, would correct that 'error of our predecessors' by 'assuming the duty of preventing infractions'.[8] In a subsequent letter to his constituents in Minas Gerais, Vasconcellos praised the judicial office which 'in England is so well regarded that it is sought by peers, the chancellor, and even by princes of the blood', urging his compatriots to choose good men for the post and thus 'imitate England, and we will gain the same benefits'.[9]

The law of 15 October 1827 did give the local elective judge jurisdiction over minor civil disputes as well as broad powers to exercise vigilance over his jurisdiction, break up illegal gatherings, collect evidence of crimes and arrest

---

geográphico e ethnográphico do Brasil, vol. 1, pp. 1107–87 (Rio de Janeiro, 1922), p. 1119.
[6] Luiz Gonçalves dos Sanctos, *Memórias para servir à história do reino do Brazil*, 2 vols. (Lisbon, 1825), vol. 1, pp. 73, 93–4.
[7] For study of the ideological debates and political manoeuvring surrounding the justice of the peace proposal see Thomas Flory, *Judge and Jury in Imperial Brazil, 1808–1871* (Austin, 1981).
[8] Brazil, *Anais da Câmara dos Deputados*, 28 June 1827, p. 178
[9] Bernardo Pereira de Vasconcellos, *Manifesto político e exposição de princípios* (Brasília, 1978), p. 88.

and judge violators. Whatever foreign models might have inspired the initiative (in addition to the British model, French and United States prototypes were discussed at the time), the mandate of the justice of the peace as both a police agent and local judge followed the Portuguese colonial tradition of combining such functions in the hands of local officials. The difference was that the authority and legitimacy of the justice of the peace would come from the people who elected him, rather than emanating from the monarch. Also like the colonial pattern, in which deliberately overlapping jurisdictions served as a sort of inefficient check on the arbitrary whims of individual office holders, the mandate of the justice of the peace overlapped in Rio with those of the intendant of police and his subordinate criminal judges.

The anomaly of an elected judge at the local level whose relationship to the appointed judicial hierarchy was left unspecified bothered some involved in the discussion of the proposal. Diogo Antônio Feijó, a member of the moderate liberal faction in parliament who later became minister of justice and regent during the minority of Pedro II, expressed such reservations during the 1827 debates and advocated a mechanism by which an appointed district judge (juiz de direito) would have the authority to review the decisions of the justices of the peace. He intended this power of oversight to make the justices more cautious in their deliberations and to spare the common people, who would have little other recourse, from arbitrary lower court rulings.10 No such clause was included in the law creating the office, but in 1831 Feijó used his authority as minister of justice to bring the justices of the peace in Rio de Janeiro into the authority structure of the central government, effectively stripping them of autonomous jurisdiction.

Few seemed quite sure in 1827 how these contradictions would be worked out in practice, and it was easier for the liberal ideologues in parliament to create a local police magistrate in principal than to establish the functioning system of vigilance and prevention that Vasconcellos wanted to see in place. What there was of the latter in Rio was left in the hands of the intendant and the *juizes do crime*, posts which were not affected by the law creating the justice of the peace. Like his appointed predecessors, the justice of the peace was authorised to call up the militia in times of crisis. He was also authorised to appoint civilian ward inspectors (*inspetores de quarteirâo*) in his jurisdiction, unpaid part-time volunteers who were to assist in local surveillance. But without control over a functioning police force, the justice of the peace had no coercive instrument by which to carry out his police mandate.

In any case, the first holders of the office in Rio de Janeiro were not elected until 1830. The new institution first achieved some public prominence in the capital in March and April the following year, during the

---

10 Brazil, *Anais da Câmara dos Deputados*, 28 June 1827, p. 176.

political crisis surrounding the abdication of Pedro I. In March 1831 gangs of radical nativists began to wage sporadic battles with pro-Portuguese toughs on the streets of Rio. Minister of Justice Manoel José de Souza França called the recently-elected justices of peace in the city together and instructed them to patrol their districts as police. In their support, the minister ordered loyal infantry and cavalry troops to be stationed at strategic points, at the disposal of the justices of the peace.[11] Thus the first major initiative to exercise the powers vested in the elected judges came from the Ministry of Justice, as did the troops to back up the local judges' authority. When a crowd of several thousand soldiers and citizens converged on the Campo de Santana on 6 April, the justices of the peace, who were among the few holders of public office not beholden in some way to the emperor, emerged as 'popular' leaders. A delegation of the justices presented Pedro I with the crowd's demands that he appoint a 'Brazilian' ministry to replace his pro-Portuguese advisors. His refusal precipitated the abdication, in the early hours of 7 April. A similar group of JPs participated in the acclamation of his five-year-old successor that same afternoon.[12]

The law of 6 June 1831

In the course of consolidating emergency measures subsequent to the abdication, the functional role of the justices of the peace was changed fundamentally from the theoretical ideals the reformers envisioned in the mid-1820s. The very first law the parliament approved upon convening after the abdication, on 6 June 1831, gave the central government broad powers to define and maintain public order. This law marked the beginning of conservative centralisation, at least at the level of local judicial authority, and it clearly subjected the justices of the peace to central control. It was an explicitly transitory measure, but it set a tone and direction, as well as several important institutional precedents.[13] Several provisions had the appearance of strengthening the power of the justice of the peace, who was given authority over public order crimes (such as illegal assembly, weapons possession, disturbing the peace) and the power to appoint a deputy (*delegado*) and up to six officers to form a proto-police staff in each of the 16 judicial

---

[11] Brazil, *Relatório do Ministro da Justiça*, 1831, p. 3. The street battles of mid-March 1831 are known as the 'nights of the bottle-throwing' (*noites das garrafadas*).
[12] Neill Macaulay, *Dom Pedro: The Struggle for Liberty in Brazil and Portugal, 1798–1834* (Durham, 1986), pp. 250–1; Roderick Barman, *Brazil, The Forging of a Nation, 1798–1852* (Stanford, 1988), p. 159; Jean Baptiste Debret, *Viagem pitoresca e histórica ao Brasil* (2 vols.) (São Paulo, 1978), vol. 2, pp. 334–5.
[13] The text of the law, on which the following discussion is based, is in *Coleção das Leis do Brasil — Atos do Poder Legislativo*, 6 June 1831, part 1, pp. 1–4.

districts of the city. An apparently minor gesture, nonetheless establishing an important symbol of civilian police authority, provided for a distinctive regalia for these officers 'so that they may be recognised, respected, and obeyed'. Anyone falsely using such a badge to impersonate a judicial officer was to spend three months in prison. (A decree of 14 June specified that the justice of the peace would wear a shoulder-to-waist sash one span [*palmo*, about eight inches] wide, of one yellow band bordered by two green bands. His deputy would wear a similar sash of one yellow and one green band.)[14] However, following this expansion of the police personnel directly under the JP, the intendant of police and the existing criminal judges, plus two additional criminal judges created by this law for Rio de Janeiro — all agents of the central government — were given the same authority over public order offences as were given to the justices of the peace. These intentionally overlapping jurisdictions gave the government the right to step in and take over from the justices of the peace in such cases as the government deemed necessary. More directly, the central government could by this law suspend any justice of the peace found guilty of malfeasance (an offence elaborately defined in article 129 of the 1830 Criminal Code) or negligence, and any judge who failed to proceed 'with the necessary diligence' in the prosecution of public order crimes was to be held as an accomplice to the offence in question.

A few weeks later, on 5 July, the regency government appointed a minister of justice ready and willing to put these laws into effect: Diogo Antônio Feijó. He quickly became the strongest figure at a weak moment in the political history of Brazil, whose actions in resolving a series of crises during the year he was minister of justice left a lasting imprint on the police and judicial system of Rio de Janeiro. As one contemporary chronicler noted, the first order of business for the regency was to choose a firm and capable minister of justice, the person responsible for the public tranquility so constantly disturbed, and the personal safety of the citizens '... continuously threatened, insulted, persecuted, and abused by actions of the lowest rabble, who had taken over the streets and squares, and stirred up frequent disorders there. [In Feijó] a more appropriate minister could not have been chosen in that troubled period, clouded by the most subversive theories and constantly shaken by anarchic disturbances and dangerous disorders'.[15]

Feijó's mettle was soon put to the test. In mid-July 1831, the capital city was thrown into upheaval as a full army batallion declared itself in revolt and was joined by the Guarda Real de Polícia, the city's uniformed patrol force since 1809. For more than a week the city was not policed, no judicial authority was exercised, and the risk of lessened control was directly confirmed, as

---

[14] *Coleção das Leis do Brasil — Atos do Poder Executivo*, part 1, 14 June 1831, p. 15.
[15] J. M. Pereira da Silva, *História do Brazil de 1831–1840* (Rio de Janeiro, 1878), pp. 20–1.

political anarchy precipitated rampant criminality and personal insecurity.[16] In the immediate aftermath of the events of July 1831, Feijó took several interim measures — all without precedent in the untried authority of the regency, and all intended to centralise power in the hands of the government and re-establish control over the streets of the city. On 20 July Feijó declared that any justice of the peace who declined to bring charges against those involved in the vanquished rebellion would himself be held accountable as an accomplice under the law of 6 June. He further ordered the justices of the peace of the city of Rio to attend weekly meetings presided over by the intendant of police, to exchange information on the possibility of revolutionary plots and coordi-nate their response to threats to public tranquility.[17] This was one of several measures of the early regency bringing the justices of the peace in Rio under the direct control of the central government.

In October 1831 a new uniformed patrol force was authorised for the capital city, replacing the Guarda Real which was abolished after its members joined the military rebels in mid-July. Feijó himself issued the instructions for the new police (the Corpo Municipal de Permanentes, direct institutional predecessor of today's Polícia Militar), entered into the order of the day on 29 November 1831 along with instructions to begin patrol duty immediately. Those detained were to be taken before the justice of the peace one day, the criminal judge the next day, and the intendant of police on the third day, in rotation. This provision was intended to relieve any one of these authorities from the need to be on duty constantly, but it also reflected the way justices of the peace in Rio had been incorporated into the lower reaches of the centrally controlled judicial system by this early date, indistinguishable in this lower criminal court function from the intendant and criminal judge. Furthermore, it reflected the transitory nature of the institutional structure at the juncture of 1831, with three judicial officials of different origins and mandates given overlapping and interchangeable functions. Within a year the code of criminal procedure would abolish the post of intendant of police, and the justices of the peace were stripped of their authority over police and criminal matters less than a decade later in favour of appointed judges.

The code of criminal procedure

A clearly organised criminal code of 1830 had superseded the jumble of codes, laws and regulations inherited from the colony, but the unsettled en-vironment of 1831–32 was hardly conducive to making much progress to-wards the next step in replacing the colonial judicial system: establishing the institutions and processes by which the criminal code could be applied. In

---

[16] For details on the events of July 1831, see Thomas Holloway, *Policing Rio de Janeiro: Re-pression and Resistance in a 19th-Century City* (Stanford, 1993), pp. 67–82.
[17] Da Silva, *História do Brazil de 1831–1840*, p. 28.

the interim the first emperor had abdicated, the old police force in Rio had been dissolved, a new one established, and in matters relating to public security and criminal offences the justices of the peace had been brought under the effective control of the minister of justice. The institutional transition would not be complete, however, without a new code of criminal procedure.

That law, approved in November 1832, swept aside the overlapping and vaguely defined judicial positions inherited from the old regime. It set up a new hierarchy of judges with circumscribed jurisdictions; laid out the procedure for gathering evidence, lodging complaints, effecting arrests and bringing charges specified how trials were to be conducted and the steps to appeal. The rights of those suspected or accused were protected through provisions for search only on a judicial warrant, arrest only on a warrant or *in flagrante*, confirmation of the writ of *habeas corpus*, trial in open court with cross-examination of witnesses, and similar guarantees. Provisions for Brazil's first jury system for serious crimes fulfilled another liberal promise of the 1824 Constitution. Certainly by comparison to the old regime in Brazil, but also in comparison to the range of analogous systems then extant in Europe, and the relative state of judicial anarchy reigning through much of Spanish America in 1832, the code of criminal procedure together with the earlier criminal code gave Brazil a set of modern and liberal guidelines regarding judicial institutions and processes.[18]

The central figure in the structure in the established procedural code was the justice of the peace. The law specified the authority of the local judges to exercise local police functions and judge minor offences. These were defined as violations of municipal ordinances and crimes punishable by a fine up to $100,000, or a prison term of up to six months with a fine of half that amount. Each justice was to be assisted by a legal clerk (*escrivâo*) who was to draw up all necessary documents for the exercise of the judge's authority, and who, as an officer of the court, could serve legal papers. The local judge was also assisted by ward inspectors (*inspetores de quarteirâo*). This latter office had been authorised in the 1827 law creating the justices of the peace, abolished by the law of 6 June 1831, and then reintroduced with qualifications and duties newly specified in the procedural code. The local judge was to divide his district into subsections of at least 25 residences each (each a contiguous area, but related only figuratively to a physical city block bounded by four streets), and nominate an inspector for each ward from among the 'well regarded' residents over 21 years of age, for confirmation by the municipal council. They were to keep an eye out for illegal or suspicious activity in their ward, warn beggars, vagrants, drunks and prostitutes to change their ways or suffer further legal action, arrest *in flagrante*, and carry out the orders of the justice

---

[18] The procedural code is in *Coleçâo das Leis do Brasil — Atos do Poder Legislativo*, 29 Nov. 1832, pp. 155–99.

of the peace. The position of *delegado*, the assistant to the justice of the peace authorised on 6 June 1831, was abolished.

The procedural code specified that the basic unit of the judicial structure would be the justice of the peace district, each of which was to have a minimum of 75 residences. The next larger jurisdiction was the *termo* made up of more than one JP district. Each *termo* was to have a municipal judge and a public prosecutor. The municipal judge was appointed by the city council, was not required to have legal training, and was authorised only to 'exercise police jurisdiction cumulatively' with the justice of the peace. In other words, the appointed municipal judge's authority overlapped with that of the elected JP. Next larger was the *comarca*, in each of which there was to be a district judge (*juiz de direito*) appointed by the emperor (in practice by the minister of justice), from among men who were at least 22 years old, were graduates of law school, and had at least one year of experience practising law. They were given several important responsibilities, including the obligation to 'inspect the justices of the peace and municipal judges, instructing them in their duties when necessary'. This followed an earlier recommendation by Feijó, who had urged as early as 1827 that justices of the peace be put under the authority of appointed judges. In May 1832, at the time the procedural code was being drafted, Feijó praised the zeal of the justices of the peace in acting against common criminals, but lamented that JPs were allowed to exercise independent judicial authority, because many of the part-time lay judges were not prepared to exercise such a responsibility. He urged that 'honest and intelligent magistrates' be appointed by the government, 'with cumulative jurisdiction and inspection over the justices of the peace'. In view of both political disruption and common criminality, such a measure would 'enable the government to ensure public tranquillity and safety.[19] This proposal was subsequently incorporated into the procedural code, included as attributes of the municipal and district judges.

One of the last vestiges of the pre-independence judicial system, the office of police intendant, was eliminated by the new code. The clerical staff he had administered, along with the records of the intendancy, were turned over to a newly created office, that of chief of police. The procedural code provided that 'in populous cities there can be up to three district judges, with cumulative [i.e., overlapping] jurisdiction, and one of them will be the chief of police'. It is indicative of the little concern the writers of the law gave the office of police chief, that they did not specify its rights and responsibilities, nor its relationship to other police and judicial authorities. By all accounts the framers did not think through the implications of replacing the intendant with a chief of police, but it turned out to be a momentous precedent. Rio's police chief emerged as an important figure in the decade following promulgation of the

---

[19] Brazil, *Relatório do Ministro da Justiça* (1832), pp. 5–6.

code, and police chiefs in each province had acquired great power and importance throughout Brazil by the judicial reform of 1841.

Before appointing a permanent occupant to the position in Rio, the minister of justice tried to fill the gap with a regulatory decree specifying that the police chief was to serve as a liaison between the government and the justices of the peace, but the wording of the procedural code did not allow for much more than that. In frustration, the minister said in May 1833 that 'a better organised police is indispensable. The justices of the peace cannot carry out the task satisfactorily, and one cannot put the uniformed police units at the disposition of so many judges without the loss of the necessary unity'. As minimally outlined in the procedural code, he went on, '"police chief" is a meaningless title that only serves to burden the judge who holds it'. He anticipated that the public would expect the office to function like that of the former intendant, but that would be an illusion because the police chief 'does not have the authority to issue a single search warrant, nor even one arrest warrant'.[20] What he did have, however, was the power and authority of the district judge, for holding that office was a prerequisite for appointment as chief of police.

The man appointed as Rio's first permanent police chief, Eusébio de Queiroz, an untested but well-connected 20-year-old lawyer, made much more of the office than more senior political figures imagined it would be, by applying disparate provisions of the procedural code in ways its writers had not envisioned. The formative experience in Queiroz's public life was his long tenure as Rio's police chief, from 27 March 1833 to 20 March 1844.[21] When he took the position there was no precedent for its functioning. Although Feijó had incorporated the JPs into the centrally controlled institutional network during 1831–32, they retained responsibility for supervising police activity at the local level. In July of 1833, early in his long tenure as police chief, Queiroz had been given control over the operating budgets of the justices of peace in those activities relating to policing the city, as part of the general liaison function of his new post.[22] That role put him in frequent contact with the JPs and the many local problems on the streets. And in working with the ministers of justice and their staffs he

---

[20] Brazil, *Relatório do Ministro da Justiça* (1833), pp. 21–2

[21] Queiroz was younger than the minimum age stipulated for district judges in the procedural code, but that was apparently overlooked in view of his record — he was a graduate of the first class of the new law school in Recife, and was already serving as a criminal judge in 1832 — and his family connections. Eusébio's father was a distinguished jurist of the late colonial era, and served on Brazil's highest court, the Supremo Tribunal de Justiça, from the time it was established in 1829 until his death in August 1842. There was a six-month hiatus in Eusébio Queiroz's tenure as police chief in 1840–41, occasioned by his political disagreements with the liberal group promoting the premature declaration of the majority of Pedro II. The measure for which Queiroz is best known as politician and minister of justice is the law which in September 1850 declared the transatlantic slave trade to be piracy; see Leslie Bethell, *The Abolition of the Brazilian Slave Trade* (Cambridge, 1970), pp. 339–41.

[22] Arquivo Nacional do Rio de Janeiro (hereafter cited as ANRJ) IJ6 166 (*Ofícios do Chefe de Polícia da Corte*), 3 July 1833.

developed an appreciation of the objectives of the government and the means available to build the sort of coordinated police apparatus that could reduce the inefficiencies of the decentralised structure.

By adopting modern administrative structures, those members of society with property and position to defend used some of their collective resources to hire and direct a professional police and local judicial system exercising complementary functions. This proved to be a lasting combination, but it took some adjustment to get there from the institutional environment of 1833. Brazilians had eliminated the formal structures of the old regime in their capital city, but colonial administrative traditions were harder to extirpate. According to the practices of the colonial era, with the source of authority thousands of miles away and the purpose of the colony to serve masters elsewhere, overlapping functions and vague lines of authority were a way of providing a primitive bureaucratic backup system, in a similar way to technological redundancy in a modern spacecraft sent beyond the reach of those who build it. If one institution or individual failed, another was able to step in as replacement. Furthermore, if two colonial authorities had overlapping functions, the competitive defence of prerogatives might provide the incentive for a certain level of performance in the system as a whole. One of the costs was the expenditure of energy and attention on rivalry among parts of the system, at the expense of efficiently accomplishing the original objectives the Portuguese colonial administrators had in mind.

This administrative tradition was still seen in several of the institutional innovations of the first empire and regency period, when some officials were formally given 'cumulative', i.e., overlapping functions with others. For example, the elected justices of the peace in Rio were brought into the centrally controlled judicial hierarchy by giving appointed judges — first the intendant and criminal judge and, with the 1832 procedural code, the municipal and district judges — authority and duties that overlapped and had precedent over those of the elected justice of the peace. Experience showed that the costs that those in the centre of the vast and scattered Portuguese empire had borne in order to administer the colonies in former times were more than the men who ran Rio de Janeiro wanted or needed to bear in the new state. They learned that institutional redundancy was more trouble than it was worth, and with direct control it was preferable to separate functions and duties into discrete and manageable units.

Revolt of the kettle makers

A tragic incident occurred in 1833, early in the history of the judicial structure of the regency, involving a JP and the paramilitary national guard: the former ignored and the latter responded to the call of a man looking for assistance in keeping the slaves in his charge in line. It reflects the sort of administrative inefficiency which higher officials increasingly blamed on unreliable JPs who, many political authorities believed, too often saw fit to act on their presumed prerogative as the only elected members of the judicial hierarchy. It is also one of the few recorded examples of slave rebellion in the city of Rio in the nineteenth century.

On the evening of 14 April 1833, Rodrigo Pinto da Costa, foreman of a kettle factory at No. 70 Alfândega street, was surprised when some of the slaves he supervised objected to routine disciplinary punishment. Early the next afternoon Costa visited Gustavo Adolfo de Azevedo, justice of the peace in the district where the shop was located, and asked for help, saying he feared an 'uprising' of the slaves in the workshop. Azevedo suggested that Costa should appeal to the uniformed police patrols if necessary to control insubordinate slaves, because as justice of the peace he could only arrest persons accused of crimes. Disciplinary punishment, the judge reminded the foreman, could be administered at the old slave jail, the Calabouço, at Costa's request. Later on the afternoon of 15 April Costa attempted to take into custody those slaves he considered a threat, but they refused to submit, arming themselves instead with tools from the shop. At 5 p.m. the impasse came to a head when the slaves forced Costa from the premises and locked themselves inside. Costa called for help from the National Guard, the citizens' militia that had been established in 1831, and finding justice of the peace Azevedo away from home, he appealed to the justice from the adjacent district to intervene.

Antônio Alves da Silva Pinto Jr., justice of the peace of the adjacent second district of Candelária, arrived on the scene about 7 p.m., and found the 14 slaves of the kettle shop engaged in a 'dangerous and threatening uprising', barricaded in a storage room in the back of the establishment. The doorway leading to their refuge was being watched by an armed national guard detachment that had responded to Costa's earlier alarm call. The foreman led Pinto to an upstairs room which looked out over the courtyard and the storage area where the slaves had barricaded themselves. Pinto tried to talk the rebels into surrender, to no avail. The ensuing sequence of events is best related in Pinto's own words:

> With peaceful means exhausted, I warned the rebels that there was a large force prepared to repress and contain them, against which their number and strength would be powerless. To this they replied that 'we will die when we can kill no more'. I told them that despite their stubbornness they would be arrested in any event, and that they could give themselves up when the exit was secured. I then positioned the armed men so as to avoid confusion and maintain calm, giving orders that only an extreme emergency could justify the use of force and that once the passage was opened a new warning would bring the rebels under control.

> As it happened, however, when this final warning was passed to the rebels and they were told to come out one by one, they charged out as a group,

attacking with hatchets, knives, hammers, stones, bars, and other weapons from among the tools used in the workshop. At that point the national guardsmen opened fire in self-defence. I ordered them to cease immediately, and only six or seven shots were fired. As a result the leader of the rebels, who was in front of the group, was killed by a bullet. Some of the others were wounded when, even after being subjugated by force, they engaged in violent resistance in attempting to escape.

Justice of the peace Azevedo, to whom Costa had appealed in vain during the first stages of the slaves' recalcitrance, soon arrived on the scene. He found Calixto, leader of the revolt, dead, the other 13 slaves on their way to jail, and calm restored.[23]

There were several lessons to be learned from this incident. For urban slaves, it confirmed the difficulty of mounting concerted resistance to their condition, and it helps explain why there are not more of such incidents on record.[24] While plantation slavery was maintained by the immediate presence of the slave driver and whatever force the planter deemed necessary, the urban master had the coercive power of the state close at hand. In the city the slave owner had an obligation to himself and the surrounding society to maintain the first line of slave discipline, but short of constant imprisonment owners could not be expected to be in direct control of their slaves at all times. As a minister of justice said of the problem of controlling slaves in the city, 'one does not guard this property, it walks through the streets'.[25] In a city where thousands of captive people were in easy communication, the threat of slave resistance or worse was too important to be left to individual owners. A system of vigilance, control and discipline had been built up to such an extent that the coercive power of the owner class was pervasive. To expect slaves to engage in open rebellion in such an environment is to expect them to act irrationally, if we assume it was rational for them not to want to suffer intense and prolonged pain, to languish in foetid dungeons, or to die. There came a time for Calixto and his companions when rational action was measured by other criteria. Their final decision, as they prepared to leave this life, was to take as many of their oppressors with them as they could.[26]

---

[23] ANRJ GIFI 5B 517, 16 May 1833.

[24] Mary Karasch discusses the apparent absence of violent slave rebellion in Rio in *Slave Life in Rio de Janeiro, 1808–1850* (Princeton, 1987), pp. 323–31, including the explanation that control was tight.

[25] Brazil, *Relatório do Ministro da Justiça*, 1833, p. 24. The flexibility of urban slavery relative to the regimentation of the plantation is assessed in Emíia Viotti da Costa, *Da senzala à colônia*, (São Paulo, 1966), pp. 227–40; and Kátia Mattoso, *Ser escravo no Brasil* 2nd ed. (São Paulo, 1988), pp. 141–3, 147–8.

[26] This is not to reduce the incident to the simplistic criteria of functionalist 'rational choice' game theory, but to suggest that rationality is relative. For commentary on this issue see James Scott, 'Resistance without Protest and without Organization: Peasant Opposition to the Islamic *Zacat* and the Christian Tithe', *Comparatives Studies in Society and History*, vol. 29, no. 3 (July 1987), p. 450.

There is another element of Calixto's revolt that merits attention. The slaves were being disciplined not simply to enforce some abstract social hierarchy or because foreman Costa was a cruel person, but so that they would make the kettles upon which Costa's salary and his employer's profits depended. One reason to try to prevent an escalation of events to the level they reached was that the production of pots was stopped, at least temporarily, and the proprietor suffered considerable direct loss when Calixto was killed and the rest of his workers were carted off to jail. Even if their punishment was to be whipped with the hundreds of lashes usual for such offences, and they survived that treatment, and were returned to their owner, his business had suffered. Control over the behaviour of the slaves and the non-slave lower classes of Rio de Janeiro could not be total or absolute, and the unrestrained application of arbitrary brutality would have been counterproductive, in the literal sense. The political theories that were helping Europeans redefine the relationship between the individual and the state in that era, and which were so talked about in Brazilian political circles, were of little help in redefining the relationship between master and slave. The contradictions of authoritarian liberalism were laid bare in the doorway of the kettle shop on Alfândega street as Calixto lay dying from a musket ball of the citizen's militia.

Few people understood this need to refine the techniques of repression better than Diogo Antônio Feijó. In addition to his instrumental role in recentralising the lower level judicial system during his term as minister of justice in 1831–32, he had issued a series of orders defining the relationship between the emerging state and the slave owner, as they divided the task of enforcing discipline. In October 1831 he ordered that the whipping of slaves in the Calabouço should not exceed a total of 200 lashes for each offence, and as specified in the 1830 Criminal Code the maximum per day would not exceed 50 lashes. Feijó also ordered that correctional punishment in the Calabouço at the request of the slave owner was not to exceed a total of 50 lashes, 'since more than 50 should be understood as excessive punishment, and thus prohibited by law'. Feijó made a telling statement justifying these limits on disciplinary whippings, and determining that 'the authority of the slave owner, restricted to the correction of minor faults, should not be extended to punishment for crimes which are under the jurisdiction of the judicial system. Slaves are men, and the law extends to them'.[27]

The developing state, with these and related measures, increasingly entered into the area of slave-master relations, imposing the rule of law and attempting to limit arbitrary and excessive physical abuse in order to preserve a system thus considered to be more humane. The apparent compas-

---

[27] '*Os escravos são homens, e as leis os compreendem*'. Brazil, *Relatório do Ministro da Justiça*, 1832, p. 11. The regulations of the Calabouço are in ANRJ IJ6 165, 15 Oct. 1831, and ANRJ IJ6 173, 2 Aug. 1836.

sion of Feijó in this passage must be understood in the context of the maintenance of an ideological system and a legal culture that could consider the
slave to be a human being, and at the same time regulate brutal techniques
of repression and maintain slavery itself. Being 'human' in nineteenth-
century Brazil was not inconsistent with being bought, sold, bound, chained,
whipped, thrown into dungeons, having irons clamped on one's neck and
leg.[28] For Feijó and like-minded authoritarian liberals, the rule of law, which
also meant the authority of the state, should extend into the realm of public
behaviour of slaves, meeting the authority of the slave owner at the door of
his private domain.

From the standpoint of the system of repression more narrowly defined,
there were also lessons to be learned from the revolt of the kettle makers.
That system was adjusted through time in response to a cumulative assessment of many minor incidents. But such outbursts as the one Calixto and his
co-workers precipitated in 1833 gave special urgency to such apparently technical and institutional matters as the lines of authority connecting elected JPs
and other parts of the appointed judicial hierarchy. Specifically, if Justice of
the Peace Azevedo had been more responsive to foreman Costa's first call for
assistance, the affair might not have reached its fatal impasse later that night.
Instead he told Costa it was out of his jurisdiction, and the beleaguered foreman eventually got a group of national guardsmen to come to his aid as his
problem escalated. By the accounting of the second JP eventually brought
from the neighbouring jurisdiction, the undisciplined guardsmen disobeyed
his orders to exercise restraint, and when the smoke cleared Calixto lay dead.

In such a complicated institutional environment some coordination became necessary, and Eusébio de Queiroz used the new office of chief of police
to provide it. As the decade wore on, coordination grew to resemble control,
as the police chief became increasingly powerful at the expense of the putative
independence of the locally elected JPs. By 1837, as he entered his mid-
twenties, Queiroz began of his own volition to take many routine decisions
affecting the operation of the JPs, including mediating disputes among
judges, based on the body of precedent then building. As district judge he had
authority to overrule any judicial action by any JP, but the administrative procedures had to be established anew after the promulgation of the procedural
code. As Queiroz took an activist stance on these city-wide issues his standing
grew in the eyes of higher officials, and he was ordered to exercise effective
supervision over the JPs. In early 1838, for example, Bernardo Pereira de
Vasconcellos, then minister of justice, instructed the police chief to make sure

---

[28] Richard Graham's assessment of the 'family paradigm' governing both personal and political hierarchies helps explain the apparent contradictions of Feijó's 'humanitarianism': 'No
dichotomy existed between force and benevolence: Each drew its meaning from the other.
They simply represented two aspects of the same technique for controlling others'. *Patronage
and Politics in Nineteenth-Century Brazil* (Stanford, 1990), p. 24.

that JPs did not grant release on bail in cases in which it was not allowed, or circumstances did not warrant. If he found such cases Queiroz, in his capacity as police chief and district judge, was to overrule the derelict JP. [29]

An incident in 1838 reflected sharp conflict between neighbouring judges, and the inefficiencies of policing a city divided into discrete judicial districts. The justice in the first district of Glória parish sharply accused his colleague in the second district of egregiously violating principles of territorial jurisdiction, when the latter called upon police soldiers at a guard post straddling the boundary of their respective districts to assist him in surveillance and arrests. The justice of the second district replied that although the guardpost in question was technically located within the first district, it had been placed in the area 'to assist justice', and that because of the easy passage from one zone to the other, along with the increased vigilance necessary 'on Sundays and holidays', he had requested the soldiers to increase patrols and stop and search suspect individuals in his own second district, in combination with their action in the first district. The soldiers had complied. The problem came from the injured prerogatives of the first district JP. Queiroz ruled that the police soldiers should be on call to either justice for tasks in their respective districts, particularly in cases of hot pursuit of suspects passing from one jurisdiction to the other.[30] In this case Queiroz, the mediating authority, resolved the dispute following principles of efficient vigilance and control, rather than yielding to the sectarian complaints of a local judge.

The judicial reform of 3 December 1841

Just as the introduction of the elective local judgeship was a significant innovation in 1827, its marginalisation in 1841 was an important change from the standpoint of the political philosophy and ideologies orienting the institution-building efforts of the first empire and regency. But in Rio de Janeiro, the nation's capital and the urban venue most directly relevant to the idealistic liberal reformers and pragmatic conservatives making the laws, the justices of the peace never threatened the stability of centralised control, and only briefly, in the uncertain climate of 1830–31, did they have even the potential for autonomous action. The local justices in Rio were subordinated to the authority of the minister of justice by the first law of the regency, in June 1831, and as the 1832 Procedural Code was put into place, the JP became subordinate in practice to the city's appointed police chief. Supreme in his jurisdiction at the age of 29 in 1841, Eusébio de Queiroz was referred to in Parliament as a 'police celebrity, whose gaze penetrates everything'.[31] He

---

[29] ANRJ IJ6 186, 23 Jan. 1838.
[30] ANRJ IJ6 187, 27 Aug., 10 Sept. 1838.
[31] Brazil, *Anais da Câmara dos Deputados* 1841, session of 20 July 1841, p. 264.

advocated and implemented the system by which parish-level judicial authorities became part of the appointed hierarchy. As early as 1834 the minister of justice had called for a centralised system, by making the JP an appointive office. That change also became a pet project of conservative minister Bernardo Pereira de Vasconcellos, the same man who in 1827, as a member of what was then called the liberal faction in Parliament, had advocated establishing the elected justice of the peace as a 'police magistrate'.[32] From the perspective of national-level politicians, the justice of the peace had proved a nearly unmitigated failure as the basis for a system for controlling unlawful activity. The locally elected judge was a principal casualty of the reform, but the office had by that time become thoroughly discredited in influential political circles. As the minister of justice put it in 1840, while advocating the reform approved the following year, 'police agents are the front line organs of government, who are party to the confidential workings of the state and authorised to use force. To have them elected independently of the government, or even contrary to the wishes of the government, is certainly an anomalous, if not an absurd, institution'.[33] In short, in the area of local judicial power, the political elite of Brazil concluded that electoral democracy was incompatible with the interests of the state. The centralised procedures that had been established in Rio during the 1830s, subordinating the justices of peace to the authority of the chief of police, provided a model for a system that was, by the law of 3 December 1841, formally secured and extended in principle over the entire country. After December 1841, stripped of all police authority and of nearly all authority in civil cases, the justice of the peace became a vestigial remnant of the original 1827 model.[34]

The new national structure was to have a chief of police in each province, and in Rio de Janeiro as national capital, appointed by the emperor (in practice by the minister of justice) from among those district judges with at least 3 years experience on the bench. The police chief of the city of Rio de Janeiro reported directly to the minister of justice, as Queiroz had been

---

[32] Brazil, *Anais da Câmara dos Deputados*, 1841, vol. 3, pp. 627, 664, 725; Barman, *Brazil*, pp. 200–201, 207, 213; R. Graham, *Patronage and Politics*, p. 53.

[33] Brazil, *Relatório do Ministro da Justiça*, 1840, p. 15.

[34] Justices of the peace continued to preside on the boards supervising local elections, and were still charged with helping reduce the incidence of drunks and beggars on the streets. They could also adjudicate minor civil disputes, something like a small claims court; *Coleção das Leis do Brasil — Atos do Poder Legislativo*, 1841, pp. 75–95 [law of 3 Dec. 1841]. One reason the office of justice of the peace was not completely abolished was that it was established in principle by the Constitution of 1824, and its extinction would have required a constitutional change; Brazil, *Anais da Câmara dos Deputados* 1841, vol. 3, p. 705. An annotated compendium of the major laws and regulations on police and judicial matters, from the Code of Criminal Procedure of 1832 through the reform of 3 December 1841 and the next reform in September 1871, is Araujo Filgueiras Júnior, *Código do Processo do Império do Brazil*, 3 vols. (Rio de Janeiro, 1874). Thomas Flory provides a litany of complaints about the justice of the peace in practice in *Judge and Jury*, pp. 131–6.

doing since 1833. He nominated his subordinate *delegados* and *subdelegados* for formal appointment by the emperor. The *delegados* and *subdelegados*, in turn, nominated neighbourhood ward inspectors for approval by the police chief. In the apt words of the nineteenth-century liberal legal scholar Tavares Bastos, the law of 3 December 1841 'established a centralising apparatus, which descends from the emperor to the ward inspector'.[35]

Along with the centralisation of the authority hierarchy, the most significant effect of the law of 3 December was formally to extend judicial powers to the local police. Under the 1841 reform, for violation of municipal ordinances and for all misdemeanour offences, the police chiefs, *delegados*, and *subdelegados* (appointed precinct-level police authorities re-established by the judicial reform) had full authority to issue warrants for search and arrest, carry out the arrest, bring formal charges, set bail, hold summary judicial hearings, pass sentence, and supervise punishment all without the intervention of any other authority.[36] For all but the most serious crime, the police chief or his appointed delegate down to the neighbourhood level became accuser, investigator, arresting officer, prosecutor, as well as judge, jury, and jailer. As a contemporary legal scholar justified subsequent 'summary correctional or repressive police procedures', the law granting judicial authority to the police 'is useful both to society and to the accused: minor crimes, and thus minor punishments, do not require so many guarantees, nor a trial full of formalities and delays that would involve more time and expense than the matter requires'. He further explained that along with its 'criminal' function, the police had a 'correctional' function, authorising police officials to 'punish minor offences, in order to prevent them from developing into bad habits and more serious crimes'.[37]

In the jurisdiction of the national capital, extending local level judicial powers to appointed police officials was not an authoritarian innovation in violation of previous practices, as liberal critics later suggested. The intendant had been expressly granted such powers in 1808, they were transferred to the JPs in 1832, and in 1841 were passed on to the police chief and his delegates. There was considerable continuity in this regard from the en-

---

[35] Aureliano Cândido Tavares Bastos, *A província*. 2nd ed. (São Paulo, 1937) [originally published 1870], p. 110.

[36] Crimes over which the police had full jurisdiction, from investigation of the incident through to sentencing and supervising punishment, included violations of municipal ordinances (which commonly included a curfew and prohibitions on vagrancy, loitering, public drunkenness, disturbing the peace, and gambling); and all crimes with a punishment of fines up to 100 milréis; prison, banishment, or exile of up to six months, with fine corresponding to up to half that time or without additional fine; or three months in jail or public workshops, where such existed. *Coleção das Leis do Brasil — Atos do Poder Legislativo*,1832, pp. 156–7 (Article 12 of the Procedural Code); 1841, pp. 75–6, (Articles 4 and 5 of the Judicial Reform Law).

[37] José Antônio Pimenta Bueno, *Apontamentos sobre o processo criminal brasileiro*, 2nd ed. (Rio de Janeiro, 1857), pp. 4, 18–9, 186–9.

lightened despotism of the late colonial era, through the interim period of
institutional experimentation, to the centralised bureaucracy of the consolidated state. The anomaly was the 1827–41 period when locally elected
judges could exercise such authority in principle, and in Rio de Janeiro
their autonomy was soon tightly circumscribed. The effect of the 1841 reform was to restore centralised authority by removing that anomaly.

Far from being the result of vaguely shifting ideological winds, or the
simple outcome of a game of parliamentary debate, the reversal of the
glimmers of liberal legislation of 1827 (creation of the office of justice of the
peace) and 1830 (the criminal code) resulted from the conditions in the
streets of Rio. Generally under the rubric of 'alterations of public tranquility', in the euphemistic rhetoric of the time, these conditions ranged from
military sedition and mob violence, to the proliferation of urban gangs and
their depredations, to slave escapes, to an increase in personal assault and
petty theft. To those charged with maintaining order, these activities formed
a seamless continuum. The task of policing was crowd control and the suppression of armed rebellions, but it was also to maintain an environment
conducive to the business of the city, safeguard property both inanimate and
human, and make the streets safe for 'decent' citizens.

In discussing the chronology of political events, the commonality among
the range of threats to authority and hierarchy needs to be recognised. Politics was more than ideological debates and votes in parliament and newspaper editorials, and more than an alternation of armed rebellion with
discussion and negotiation. Politics involved the exercise of power, and central to the maintenance of power in the hands of a few was to defend it
against threats from the many, whether those threats are today labelled political or social. Without the masses kept in their place below, either in service and support roles or at least obedient and respectful and out of the way,
there could be no elite. The mechanisms put into place from 1831 onwards
provided the functional equivalent, adapted to the constitutional regime, of
the social repression and political control under colonial absolutism — so
hated in discourse and rejected in reform legislation. During the ensuing
decade those mechanisms were expanded and tightened in practice, leading
to another formal and legal stage of consolidation in December 1841.

Conclusions

After the judicial reform was enacted, newly empowered Police Chief Queiroz quickly moved to marginalise the JPs in his jurisdiction. The justices
were still allowed to require 'habitual drunks' to sign promises of good conduct, and to 'keep watch on their subsequent behaviour'. The standard
punishment for violation of such a promise was a jail term. When in April

1842 a JP took the next step and sentenced two men to 30 days in jail for breaking their pledge not to appear drunk in public, he went too far. Queiroz reported the violation to the minister of justice, who ruled that under the new system, 'justices of the peace may not bring charges and pass sentence ... as their police and criminal jurisdiction is very expressly and strictly limited' by the provisions of the law of 3 December and its subsequent regulations.[38] The practical effect of the 1841 judicial reform was to eliminate the elected JPs as significant cogs in the mechanism of repression, and replace them with appointed representatives of central authority.

[38] ANRJ IJ6 199, 11 May, 23 May 1842. As an example of the precedent set by such rulings originally issued locally for Rio de Janeiro, the explicit prohibition on JPs assigning jail terms, in the exact wording of the internal memo of 23 May, was subsequently issued as an *aviso* with nationwide application; see Filgueiras Júnior, *Código do Processo*, vol. 1, p. 444.

CHAPTER 5

Criminal Justice and State Formation in Early Nineteenth-Century Buenos Aires

Osvaldo Barreneche[*]

This chapter analyses changes and continuities in the administration of criminal justice of the city of Buenos Aires from the late colonial period to the mid-nineteenth century. By addressing continuities in criminal law, changes in the penal discourse, adaptation of colonial procedures and shifts in power relationships between the judiciary and law enforcement agents, the role of criminal justice during the initial stages of state formation in Argentina becomes evident.

As social scientists try to explain *how* state rule is accomplished, many of them focus on the emergence of post-independent state forms in Latin America. Some scholars, like Florencia Mallon, look at the nineteenth century to trace the origins of such forms.[1] Although the colonial past is not ignored in these cases, research efforts are concentrated on the national period. Too much emphasis on the national period, however, can obscure important continuities. Modern Latin American states did not emerge from a vacuum. In Argentina, independence was achieved during a transitional period of socioeconomic transformation from the late eighteenth to the mid-nineteenth century.[2] After 1810, when the process of Argentine independence began, institutional experimentation and adaptation of colonial state forms occurred simultaneously.

The interrelation between modified colonial state agencies and institutional experimentation after Independence can be better understood by focusing on one particular state form — criminal justice — rather than trying to deal with an Argentine 'state' that did not even exist at that time.[3]

[*] This research was assisted by grants from the Fundación Antorchas, Argentina, and the Social and Behavioral Sciences Research Institute, University of Arizona. I thank Donna Guy, the participants of the Fourth Nineteenth-Century History Workshop at ILAS, London (especially John Lynch, the commentator on my panel), and Michael Brescia for their helpful comments on earlier versions.

[1] Florencia E. Mallon, *Peasant and Nation. The Making of Postcolonial Mexico and Peru* (Berkeley, 1995).

[2] Several articles stress the significance of that historical transition in Mark Szuchman and Jonathan Brown (eds.), *Revolution and Restoration. The Rearrangement of Power in Argentina, 1776–1860* (Lincoln, 1994). The anthology by Kenneth J. Andrien and Lyman L. Johnson, *The Political Economy of Spanish America in the Age of Revolution, 1750–1850* (Albuquerque, 1994) is also relevant to this is debate.

[3] See José Carlos Chiaramonte, 'Formas de identidad en el Río de la Plata luego de 1810',

Certain aspects of criminal justice administration in the city of Buenos Aires, a key form of social mediation during the colonial period, were reformulated after Independence while others endured much longer. In such a context, it is relevant to detect explicit contrasts and accommodations between everyday judicial practices and the political struggle to redefine the state's institutional existence.

The scholarly contributions of many legal historians, lawyers and jurists in Argentina and other Latin American countries created an historiographical school based on the study of Spanish colonial legal practices and their postcolonial survival.[4] They facilitated our understanding of both colonial and 'national' penal law, but their research and conclusions were focused narrowly on general norms and codes. Emphasising the legacy of the *derecho indiano* after Independence, these *historiadores del derecho* depicted a legal context that often lacked the realities of everyday life.[5] The emergence of a post-colonial penal system in Argentina involved not only a confirmation or redefinition of colonial criminal laws but also rearrangements in the penal discourse, criminal procedures and judicial practices.[6] I will discuss these issues in order to relate the administration of criminal justice to the rise of new state forms in early independent Argentina.

Boletín del Instituto de Historia Argentina y Americana 'Dr Emilio E. Ravignani', 3rd series, vol. 1 (1989), pp. 71–92, and Chiaramonte's more recent elaboration of these ideas: 'Acerca del origen del estado en el Río de la Plata', *Anuario del Instituto de Estudios Históricos Sociales* (IEHS), no. 10 (Buenos Aires, 1995). A significant contribution to this debate is also the article by Carlos Cansanello, 'Domiciliarios y transeúntes en el proceso de formación estatal bonaerense (1820–1832)', *Entrepasados. Revista de Historia*, vol. 4, no. 6, (1994), pp. 7–22.

[4] Ricardo Levene, the doyen of this historiographical school, argued that, according to the laws, the *Indias* were not colonies. Thus, the socioeconomic historical reality of European domination in America and the colonial character of that enterprise is almost ignored. This extreme example illustrates one of the limitations of this trend in historiography, narrowly focused on legal texts and their technicalities. Ricardo Levene, *Manual de historia del derecho argentino* (Buenos Aires, 1985), pp. 25–33.

[5] Recent works on legal history in New Spain opened new perspectives on this subfield. Silvia Marina Arrom, 'New Directions in Mexican Legal History', *The Americas*, vol. 50, no. 4 (April, 1994), pp. 461–5. See also articles by Charles R. Cutter, Linda Arnold and Michael Scardaville in the same issue. Other works linking social and legal history include Michael C. Meyer, *Water in the Hispanic Southwest: a Social and Legal History, 1550–1850* (Tucson, 1984) and Charles R. Cutter, *The Legal Culture of Northern New Spain, 1700–1820* (Albuquerque, 1995).

[6] Criminologist Eugenio Raúl Zaffaroni discusses the definition and components of the penal systems. See, for example, E.R. Zaffaroni (ed.) *Sistemas penales y derechos humanos en América Latina. Informe final: documento final del programa de investigación* (Buenos Aires, 1986). See also Fernando Tocora, *Política criminal en América Latina* (Bogotá, 1990), and Martha K. Huggins (ed.), *Vigilantism and the State in Modern Latin America. Essays on Extralegal Violence* (New York, 1991).

Criminal law and penal practices

Argentine legal historians have ample evidence to highlight continuities of colonial laws after Independence. New laws, legal resolutions, and constitutional drafts recognised the applicability of previous legislation in all legal terrains including criminal justice. Actually, the first penal code was not passed in Argentina until 1886 and even after the fall of Rosas's regime in 1852 the Seventh *Partida* and other Spanish and colonial criminal laws were regularly applied. Many post-colonial laws modified the earlier legal framework but these new regulations did not totally abolish it. The *Reglamento* of 1817, for example, stated that Spanish colonial legislation would be enforced until a constitution was passed, unless they contradicted post-1810 laws or challenged the recently declared Argentine independence.[7]

Post-colonial continuities in the legal framework are less evident when we look at other types of norms and regulations, which were as significant as Spanish laws and codes in the administration of colonial criminal justice. Authorities in Buenos Aires continued using colonial *bandos* (executive decrees) to address crime-related issues after Independence, increasing the legal scope of these legal instruments. While local *bandos* during the colonial period focused on police ordinances and misdemeanours, after 1810 they also established severe punishments for certain felonies. This new legal terrain of *bando* enforcement helped to expand the power of executive authorities who enacted them.[8] These norms constituted a legal ground for the resolution of penal cases after Independence in judicial processes where colonial laws were not applied.

Liberal principles were introduced to judicial discourse soon after the first *junta* was established in 1810. At the same time, different factions in the city, competing in an environment of political turmoil and instability, wanted to use the law as a means of political legitimation. However, legitimacy (a basic premise for the consolidation of a hegemonic project) proved elusive in this situation. Colonial criminal laws (such as the Seventh *Partida*) and liberal principles (such as due process or the defendant's new individual rights) coexisted and conflicted after Independence. For example, colonial penal practices based on the *calidad* or social status of defendants and victims contradicted a discursive scenario of civic equality that was present not only in many pieces of legislation after 1810, but also in the official language of certain members of the *criollo* judiciary. As an attorney for the defence (in

---

[7] See article 2, chapter 1, section 2 of the *Reglamento Provisorio de 1817.* Emphasis on colonial-postcolonial legal continuities in Samuel W. Medrano, ' Problemas de la organización de la justicia en las primeras soluciones constituyentes', *Revista de la Facultad de Derecho y Ciencias Sociales*, vol. 9, no. 40 (Sept–Oct. 1954), pp. 1127–48.

[8] For example, an 1812 *bando* established a range of punishments in cases of burglary, conspiracy, and possession of firearms, including the death penalty. Senado de la Nación, Biblioteca de Mayo, *Colección de obras y documentos para la historia argentina*, vol. XVIII (Buenos Aires, 1966), p. 16,685.

this case *defensor de pobres*) said in 1811, judicial decisions must be based on concrete evidence 'so that human rights can be saved'.[9] Another *defensor* argued in 1813 that if there was no assurance in the verdict, punishment should be avoided because 'in criminal cases, the evidence must be as the noon light, and it is better to set the author of a crime free than condemn an innocent person'.[10] The 1813 *instrucción circular para los alcaldes de barrio*, which copied many of the articles of a similar ordinance issued during the 1790's, provides additional proof on this issue. While the colonial *instrucción* established diverse penalties for Spaniards, *mulatos*, *mestizos*, or indians, the new version said that punishments would be applied according to what the defendant did.[11] The search for political stability and the need for social control prevented the increased application of a liberal judicial discourse in the solution of everyday criminal cases. The emergence of a post-colonial criminological paradigm was debated in academic and legislative circles but this new debate had little impact on the penal system itself. Certainly, as Ricardo Salvatore argues in the case of Buenos Aires countryside, that penal system was not totally arbitrary but utilised a colonial tradition of basing decisions on socioeconomic differences characteristic of that society.[12] However, the liberal principles that supposedly constituted the base of the new system were neutralised and confined to a legal discourse in the 1853 Constitution and later in the Penal Code. Thus, these liberal principles were acknowledged but their application was deferred until better times.

In the post-independence urban scenario of Buenos Aires, many legal rights were glossed over. Technically, procedural guarantees, defendant's rights, and non-corporal punishment were not ignored but just 'postponed' in criminal cases. Diverse political factions accepted that contradiction because they believed that special political and social circumstances justified some arbitrary measures. Institutions should be first consolidated.[13] Thus, *criollo* society was not ready to appreciate the merits of a liberal system. These same pretexts subsequently justified military coups and other authoritarian experiments in Argentina.

Post-independence judicial practices shaped other theoretical conceptualisations of the 'future' Argentine penal system. Juan Bautista Alberdi,

---

[9] Archivo Histórico de la Provincia de Buenos Aires (hereafter referred to as AHPBA). Criminal Provincial, Real Audiencia y Cámara de Apelaciones, 5.5.65.44, p. 17, (1811).

[10] AHPBA, Criminal Provincial, Real Audiencia y Cámara de Apelaciones, 5.5.75.15, p. 99, (1813).

[11] ' ... para aplicarle la pena según su manejo'. Instrucción Circular para los Alcaldes de Barrio. Senado de la Nación. Biblioteca de Mayo. *Colección de obras y documentos para la historia argentina* vol. XVIII, p. 16,744.

[12] Ricardo D. Salvatore, 'El imperio de la ley: delito, estado y sociedad en la era rosista', *Delito y Sociedad, Revista de Ciencias Sociales*, vol. 3, nos. 4–5 (1993–94), pp. 93–118.

[13] 'Las instituciones aún no están consolidadas.' This was a unanimous thought among members of the 'porteño'. See, for example, the article in *El Argos de Buenos Aires* issue no. 101 (17 Dec. 1823), published by Biblioteca de la Junta de Historia y Numismática Americana (Buenos Aires, 1931–1942), pp. 413–4.

whose work was very influential in the constitutional organisation of the country after 1852, described three possible systems of judicial retribution in criminal justice: penal, penitentiary, and repressive. The penal system involved harsh punishments. It was considered less complicated but unacceptable because of its moral deficiencies. The penitentiary system attempted to stop criminal violence by eliminating its causes. It was a more humanitarian and moral system but slow and impractical. Finally, the repressive system, recommended by Alberdi in the case of Argentina, involved the specific task of neutralising criminal actions by applying diverse punishments. Some of the features of the repressive system, such as imprisonment of suspects without formal accusation, were already applied in Buenos Aires. In regular inspections of public jails, for example, judicial officials reported that neither the many prisoners nor the penitentiary authorities were able to explain why these people were there.[14]

A penal system of this kind was not the most benevolent, as Alberdi pointed out, but it was certainly the most efficient.[15] Furthermore, the repressive system was not perceived as arbitrary but as institutionally contextualised. Major inequalities in the early penal system, according to Alberdi, were due to the fact that its informal practices and procedures depended on the decision of one person: the dictator, the *caudillo*. Thus, many jurists saw a solution for the abuses of the system in the bureaucratisation of the judicial process and the hiring of more judges and judicial officials. That idea, as intellectuals recognised, was inspired in the teachings of the Italian penalist Cesare Beccaria, who remarked: 'The greater the number of judges, the less dangerous is the abuse of legal power; venality is more difficult among men who observe one another.'[16] Nonetheless, executive authorities during the 1820s, 30s and 40s, channelled substantial financial resources from Buenos Aires into the consolidation of police forces instead.

The post-colonial judiciary

In his study of social control in post-colonial Buenos Aires, Mark Szuchman points out that criminal justice in the city is best studied from police records. After analysing the adherence of police authorities to the principle of *barrio* autonomy, he concluded that the criminal justice system did not become an

---

[14] See, for example: Archivo General de la Nación (hereafter referred to as AGN), Sección Justicia, X.15.7.2, expediente suelto. Reporte del Tribunal de Justicia del 13 de mayo de 1830. Other examples in AGN X.9.1.3, Cámara de Justicia.

[15] Juan Bautista Alberdi. *Fragmento preliminar al estudio del derecho* (1837) (Buenos Aires, 1944), p. 188.

[16] Cesare Beccaria (1738–1794), *On Crimes and Punishments* (Indianapolis, 1963), p. 98. The first systematic study of Beccaria's ideas appeared in the doctoral dissertation of Florencio Varela in 1827, which, in fact, was the first dissertation on penal issues presented in the University of Buenos Aires. See Marcial Candioti, *Bibliografía doctoral de la Universidad de Buenos Aires y catálogo cronológico de las tesis en su primer centenario 1821–1920* (Buenos Aires, 1920), pp. 64–5.

integrative mechanism of nation-building in Argentina.[17] The nature of the judicial system, however, was more complex. Szuchman's focus on social control overlooks other aspects in the formation of the penal system. During the 1810s, the Rivadavian years in the 1820s, and the Rosas regime later on, spaces of power were contested and negotiated between the executive branch of the government, the judiciary and the police authorities, as well as between these state forms and diverse groups in civil society. Thus, the study of police practices of social control is relevant, but it also limits our historical understanding of the criminal justice system.[18]

The 1810s were characterised by intense, but incomplete, institutional experimentation in the definition of the functions and composition of the judiciary. During the late colonial period, the *audiencia* (appeals court) of Buenos Aires, comprised of Spanish born elite or *peninsulares*, confirmed through its sentences both the power to punish and the authority over law enforcement agents and subordinated members of the judiciary (*alcaldes*). It was common to find judicial decisions by the *audiencia* penalising someone as well as giving procedural instruction to an *alcalde* on how to handle similar cases in the future.[19] But Spanish *audiencia* members were replaced by *criollo* or native born judges after 1810 and their power and authority had to be renegotiated in less favourable conditions by the new appeals court called the Cámara de Apelaciones (known later on as the Cámara de Justicia and the Tribunal de Justicia as well). The *cámara* did not inherit many of the prerogatives of its colonial predecessor. In 1821, for instance, a law was passed that limited the power of the appeals court. It authorised oral verdicts without obligation to 'write' a judicial sentence, which eliminated the possibility of an appeal in certain cases.[20] Thus, judicial officials unsuccessfully attempted to maintain and to expand their colonial spaces of power in the decades after Independence. The Buenos Aires appeals court, along with its subordinated judges, had to rely on the police and even the military at that time to implement their resolutions. [21]

During the 1810s, diverse *criollo* governments focused on the Wars of Independence, post-colonial institutional organisation, and the debates over the legal architecture of criminal law and the judiciary. As the province of Buenos Aires was established in the early 1820s, more

---

[17] Mark D. Szuchman, 'Disorder and Social Control in Buenos Aires, 1810–1860', *Journal of Interdisciplinary History*, vol. 15, no. 1 (Summer, 1984), pp. 83–110; See also Mark D. Szuchman, *Order, Family, and Community in Buenos Aires, 1810–1860* (Stanford, 1988).

[18] Richard W. Slatta and Karla Robinson, 'Continuities in Crime and Punishment. Buenos Aires, 1820–50', Lyman L. Johnson (ed.), *The Problem of Order in Changing Societies* (Albuquerque, 1990), pp. 19–45, also principally utilised police records.

[19] For example: AHPBA, Juzgado del Crimen, 34.1.21.52, p. 16.

[20] Law passed on 27 Nov. 1821 penalising the carrying of weapons and other crimes. Aurelio Prado y Rojas (comps.), *Leyes y decretos promulgados por la provincia de Buenos Aires desde 1810 a 1876* (Buenos Aires, 1877), pp. 201–2.

[21] See, AHPBA, Criminal Provincial, 7.2.101.13, 1825.

attention was paid to the distribution of resources and procedural aspects of the penal system without necessarily benefiting a judicial power that was being reorganised at that time.[22]

In this environment, the judiciary once again did not fare well. The distribution of public revenues did not favour criminal judges and appeals courts who at the same time demanded more resources. In 1825, for example, 'imperious needs' compelled the Tribunal de Justicia to request once again increased judicial salaries to the secretary of the interior of the province of Buenos Aires (*ministro de gobierno*). Judicial employees and judges, the *tribunal* argued, had to support their families on an insufficient income which did not match 'the decorum that is implied in the judicial function'.[23]

In fact, members of the Buenos Aires appeals court could not support themselves on their judicial salaries. They often occupied other posts or had to assume additional responsibilities. Thus, they said, it was very difficult for them to concentrate on the revision of judicial criminal cases. In 1826, the president of the *tribunal* complained to the executive authorities that 'two members of the appeals court are also deputies to the General Congress'. Among the other two members of the tribunal, he said, 'one is also a provincial judge while the other is a commercial judge. On top of that, these magistrates are also being designated as special counsellors in all the martial courts. Thus, only one judge is available for judicial audiences in many cases.'[24]

During the next decade, the top provincial tribunal encountered more and more operational restrictions. Buenos Aires' appeals court depended on the decision of politicians for simple office supplies. Of the 300 pesos requested by the tribunal for everyday expenses in 1827, for example, it only received 200 pesos as of February the following year. The appeals court had to beg the governor to release the remaining 100 pesos.[25]

---

[22] For example, AGN, X.14.9.3, 14 Aug. 1828, Tribunal de Justicia al Ministro de Gobierno. In this letter, the tribunal presented its claims in the name of 'the judicial employees' which included judges and the subordinated members of the judiciary. The appeal court, in fact, exercised the superintendence of the provincial judiciary. See also AGN, X.9.1.3, Archivo de la Cámara Primera de Apelaciones, expediente 179: Ordenanzas del Tribunal o Excelentísima Cámara de Justicia. During the late 1820s and early 1830's the *Tribunal* renewed its efforts in attempting to obtain more resources and personnel from political leaders but political instability marked those transitional years from the Rivadavian liberal experiment to the Rosas regime. In that context, the Buenos Aires appeals court did not get much from the government. For the first time since Independence, however, judicial power seemed to present a more articulated voice. For the general characteristics of this transition see Tulio Halperín-Donghi, *Politics, Economics, and Society in Argentina in the Revolutionary Period* (Cambridge, 1975), especially, part two, chapter 6, pp. 308–76.

[23] 'Carta del Presidente del Tribunal de Justicia Manuel Antonio de Castro al ministro de gobierno', AGN, X.13.8.6, 29 July 1825, foja suelta.

[24] 'Nota del presidente del Tribunal de Justicia al ministro de gobierno de la Provincia de Buenos Aires', AGN, X.13.9.4, 14 Feb. 1826, foja suelta.

[25] 'Nota del Tribunal de Justicia al Ministerio de Gobierno reclamando 100 pesos faltantes de los asignados para gastos de escritorio' AGN, X.14.9.3, 27 Feb. 1828. The tribunal also depended on the executive branch of the government for other needs. I have found many re-

Negotiations over the judicial budget took place every year, provoking confrontation between the appeals court and political leaders in Buenos Aires. Once the judiciary was reorganised at the provincial level in the early 1820s, the state budget had to be approved by the legislature (Sala de Representantes). Since the judiciary was not a priority in terms of provincial expenditures, the assigned budget was usually considered inadequate and sometimes unacceptable by the appeals court. In April 1830, for example, the tribunal sent the assigned allowance back to the secretary of the interior, arguing that 'it was absolutely insufficient for covering the expenses provoked by the increasing prices'. The president of the tribunal complained that 'nobody wants to be secretary of the tribunal for 200 pesos a year, or four reales a day in actual currency. This is a miserable wage that is not enough for shoes and even for a square meal.'[26]

Responding to these complaints, the governor insisted that the provincial legislature re-evaluate the budget. Unfortunately, this strategy was a way of postponing a decision favouring the plea. Furthermore, many petitions seeking an increase in the salary of less important members of the judiciary were directly turned down by the executive authorities. As the provincial attorney general explained to the appeals court in 1827, 'the salary increase [...] cannot be considered this year. These members of the judiciary [*relatores*] are experiencing the same situation as all or most public employees and no budget modifications can be made now due to the present circumstances. The petition will be evaluated again next year'.[27]

Police budgets were a higher priority than judicial requests. The creation of new auxiliary agents working under the supervision of the urban police and the increasing expenditure of law enforcement agents during the Rosas regime in the 1830s and 1840s thus restricted a judicial budget which had never been abundant. While the office of the Buenos Aires chief of the police was equipped with fancy furniture,[28] for example, the sessions of the Tribunal de Recursos Extraordinarios created by the Rosas government had to be held in other public buildings because its own had nearly collapsed.[29] As for the Buenos Aires appeal court, its expenditure only accounted for 6 per cent of

---

quests submitted by the tribunal to the executive authorities for building repairs, new furniture, etc. See, for example, 'Nota del Tribunal del Justicia al Ministro de Gobierno requiriendo un lugar para 'los desahogos naturales' AGN, X.15.2.8, 2 Oct. 1829; or 'Pedido de reparación de una claraboya del edificio' AGN, X.9.3.1, Cámara de Justicia, 13 Sept. 1834. See also 'Nota del juez en lo criminal José Eugenio de Elías reclamando arreglos que hagan habitable este páramo' AGN, X.15.7.2, 16 June 1830.

[26] 'Expediente del Tribunal de Justicia rechazando el presupuesto asignado para el año 1830', AGN, X.15.7.2, 19 April 1830.

[27] 'Respuesta del Ministerio de Gobierno a la nota del Tribunal de Justicia solicitando aumento de sueldo para los Relatores', AGN, X.14.9.3, 18 March 1827.

[28] 'Relación de los útiles existentes en la oficina del Jefe de Policía', AGN, X.17.1.6, 31 Dec. 1838.

[29] 'Reporte sobre el lugar de reunión del Tribunal de Recursos Extraordinarios. Todas las piezas de la casa de Expósitos se hallan inservibles y amenaza ruina. Se propone su traslado', AGN, X.17.4.3, 19 Oct. 1843.

the 1847 budget while the police department alone received 29.4 per cent and the *serenos* (night watchmen), one of the auxiliary police corps, received 15.8 per cent of the public funds in the same year.[30]

Budget shortages and reduced salaries were not exclusive problems of the Tribunal de Justicia. Judges and other judicial officials relied on the appeals court to negotiate with executive authorities in Buenos Aires for better wages. The tribunal often received letters from criminal judges, prosecutors, public defendants and other judicial officials requesting improvements in their salaries, more assistant personnel and so forth. Since one of the major concerns of the diverse political factions in power after 1810 was to maintain public order through a more efficient criminal justice system, the appeal court backed up subordinate members of the judiciary by arguing that efficiency would only be accomplished with the appropriate resources.[31] Petitions for more tribunals, smaller territorial jurisdictions, and more auxiliary employees, were some of the persistent requests by judicial authorities after 1810.[32] Nonetheless, political leaders preferred to invest the few available resources in increasing the payroll and power of law enforcement agents such as the police in order to assure a certain level of social control.

Excessive police autonomy was a constant concern for judges and jurists. Many legislative projects and judicial communications reflected this apprehension. One example is a letter written by the Cámara de Justicia in 1833 introducing new plans for the administration of justice. It protested to the governor of Buenos Aires that police officers 'have become truly judges, usurping the [legal] jurisdiction that used to belong to the magistrates'.[33]

Besides their concerns over wages and budget in general, the appeal court and the judges faced specific problems stemming from the lack of human and material resources. Notifications, summonses and other judicial acts required auxiliary personnel to carry out the judges' orders. Those actions went beyond arresting someone — something usually done by the police. Judicial acts, like the ratification of witnesses' testimonies before the judge, were legal steps needed to complete a criminal case so that the final sentence could be passed by the judge or the tribunal. Prob-

---

[30] 'Resumen del presupuesto para el año 1847 presentado por el Ministerio de Gobierno', AGN, X.17.7.1, 2 Dec. 1846. Total: 2,730,196; Cámara de Apelaciones: 164,268; Departamento de Policía: 801,629.2; Departamento de Serenos: 430,632.

[31] See, for example, 'Tribunal de Justicia el Ministro de Gobierno encargándole las medidas convenientes para poner los juzgados de primera instancia en el mejor orden posible, a efectos de obtener los buenos resultados que son de desear en este ramo', AGN, X.13.8.6, 8 Jan. 1825. See also, 'Tribunal de Justicia eleva al Ministro de Goberno nota presentada por los jueces del crimen', AGN, X.15.7.2, 12 July 1830.

[32] Examples of these claims may be found in *Acuerdos del extinguido cabildo de Buenos Aires,* 21 Jan. 1817 (Buenos Aires, 1927), serie IV, volume VII, p. 441; and Report by Manuel Antonio de Castro, President of the Cámara de Justicia. *El Argos de Buenos Aires,* no. 150, (14 May 1825), publication from the Biblioteca de la Junta de Historia y Numismática Americana (Buenos Aires, 1931–1942), p. 168.

[33] 'Libro de copiar oficios', AHPBA, 1831–37, p. 64.

lems accomplishing those legal acts caused delays, reinforcing the opinions of the critics who complained of judicial inefficiency.[34]

In contrast, the police were strongly defended from criticism. An organised police force and its auxiliaries, the government stated at the same time, would constitute the executive arm of the judges and the appeals court as it had been before 1810. However, there were some differences in this regard, undermining the power of the judiciary after Independence. During the colonial period, the *alcalde* combined the judicial function of organising the *expediente* (judicial case) which the capacity for executing his own resolutions, with the help of his assistants. This last option was no longer available to post-colonial judges. They had to rely almost exclusively on the will of police and executive authorities to enforce their orders.

The Tribunal de Justicia tried to reduce this institutional dependency by limiting the police role in such judicial acts as legal notifications. In order to do this, however, the judges needed additional personnel to replace the police; this was not always possible. Criminal judges Bartolomé Cueto and Manuel Insiarte expressed the problem to the tribunal in 1828. On the one hand they acknowledged the resolution adopted by the appeals court regarding limits to police action on the execution of judicial orders. On the other hand, however, they were forced to request two additional judicial agents with horses (*ordenanzas de a caballo*) for the notifications and other legal tasks outside the courtroom. As the Tribunal de Justicia did not have the resources to enforce the resolution and satisfy the demands of the judges, once again it had to refer the request to the secretary of the interior.[35] Hence, in the long run, the judiciary was kept inside the courtroom, limiting its contact with civil society, while the police became the visible face of the penal system.

The merging of offices and functions that limited the operational capacity of the judiciary constituted an additional obstacle. The roles of public attorney for the defence, public notary, as well as other minor judicial officials were redefined several times after Independence. Reducing state expenditure rather than liberal theories motivated these changes. The merging of judicial functions was conceived, as executive authorities explained, as a temporary measure, since the positions were filled each year.[36]

Buenos Aires lawyers and other people linked to the legal profession did not always accept those appointments with enthusiasm. These positions might have helped them to strengthen their ties with the political factions in

---

[34] See, for example, the letter signed by criminal judges Manuel Insiarte and José Eugenio de Elías claiming 52 pesos per month to cover their expenses on these matters. AGN, X.15.7.2, 30 Oct. 1830.

[35] 'El Tribunal pone en manos del Señor Ministro de Gobierno la adjunta solicitud de los jueces de primera instancia en lo criminal dirijida a que se aumente una ordenanza más para los dos juzgados..., expediente suelto', AGN, X.14.9.3, 18 Aug. 1828. See also, 'Cámara de Justicia eleva pedido del juez de primera instancia en lo criminal Matías de Oliden', AGN, 9.1.3.30 bis, 2 May 1834.

[36] See, for example, 'Se reúnen los cargos de defensoría de menores y pobres y de asesor', AGN, X.15.10.3, 16 March 1831.

power, but accepting them involved a significant amount of work for a miserable salary, if they were paid at all.[37] In a letter to the secretary of the interior dated 18 December 1829, the incoming children's public defendant Victorio García Zúñiga (*defensor de menores*) reluctantly accepted the position. Ten days later, the government merged his office with that of the defendant public attorney (*defensoría de pobres*) and the office of the special public attorney for Indians (*defensoría de naturales*) for the year 1830, provoking García Zuñiga's discontent. 'During the few days I have held these positions', he argued in another letter, 'it has been absolutely impossible to deal with so many different issues and cases by myself.'[38]

Political instability during these years also meant job insecurity and precariousness in the judiciary. As they were appointed by the government, the public careers of many judicial officials were also tied to the political faction in power.[39] It is not surprising then to find judicial offices declared vacant for many years, giving another reason for merging those offices with others. In 1835, for example, the Buenos Aires appeals court reported to the government that even though several openings for the post of notary public attached to the criminal court (*escribanos del crimen*) were repeatedly announced, nobody applied.[40]

After the consolidation of Rosas's regime in 1835, the mechanisms of judicial designations were simplified in practice. Loyalty to the federal cause, certified by the executive authority, became the most important condition and the almost exclusive requirement for employment. Furthermore, if somebody could not take the post or had to leave one of these one-year judicial appointments, they were required to recommend possible replacements by suggesting other candidates' names.[41] As Jorge Myers points out, this litmus test

---

[37] The *Reglamento* for defendant public attorneys passed on 1 April 1840 explicitly stated that the person holding this office for a year was not going to receive any salary. It also established that the *defensor de pobres y menores* did not have to be a lawyer although a legally-trained assistant was also appointed for helping him. Aurelio Prado y Rojas (comp.), *Leyes, Decretos...*, volume VI, p. 361.

[38] 'Notas de Victorio García Zúñiga al ministro de gobierno', AGN, X.15.2.8, 18 Dec. 1829 and 30 Dec. 1829.

[39] When the federalists came back to power in Buenos Aires in late 1829, former prosecutor Francisco Planes petitioned for the salaries he did not get when he was fired by supporters of the 1828 triumphant unitarian revolution of Juan Lavalle. 'Judges and prosecutors were supposed to have stability in their positions', AGN, X.15.7.2, 11 June 1830.

[40] 'Vacantes en el oficio de escribano del crimen', AGN, X.16.9.3, 16 July 1835.

[41] For example, Nota del Defensor General de Pobres y Menores Joaquín Rejaval al gobernador. Publicity of executive orders in the 1830s and 1840s replaced behind-the-scene appointments of judicial officials during the 1810s and 1820s, AGN, X.17.1.6, 11 Dec. 1838. See, for example, Pedido de Antonio José de Urtubey sobre puesto de procurador vacante; AGN, 9.1.3.51, Cámara de Justicia, 28 June 1837. Rosas comunica al Tribunal de Justicia que Francisco Castellote no puede ejercer más el oficio de Escribano; AGN, 9.1.3.98, Cámara de Justicia, 25 Feb. 1840. Other cases in AGN, 9.1.3.95, Cámara de Justicia, 2 July 1840, and AGN, 9.1.3.103, Cámara de Justicia, 29 Dec. 1840.

meant that the judiciary's legitimacy did not derive from the division of power, but rather from its commitment to the regime's goals.[42]

The authority of the appeals court and criminal judges was also undermined by the creation of special judges and tribunals. Executive authorities appointed occasional judges to deal with specific felonies. The first Comisión de Justicia was created in 1812 summarily to decide all cases of theft. Its goal was to arrive at a decision 'in the shortest possible period of time' and the only procedure required was to listen to the testimony of the accused only once.[43] These special judges were appointed by the different political factions in office. In fact, justice commissions existed until the National Constitution of 1853 abolished them.[44]

Although these justice commissions and judges only acted in specific cases or times, they were resisted by the judiciary. The appeals court insisted that these special judges without formal legal training should not be appointed. As the president of the Cámara de Justicia explained in 1821, 'the quality of lawyers that is required for those who are going to serve in public office as judges is supported by the nature of their functions'.[45] Moreover, the tribunal later asserted that the opinions of these special judges often collided with the decisions of the appeals court, claiming their suppression. The existence of the justice commissions not only created a problem of diverse interpretation of the law. It also promoted a parallel system of criminal justice that was not controlled by the highest members of the judiciary, but rather by executive authorities.[46]

Criminal justice and the struggle for institutional power

During the early 1820s, the authorities of the newly created province of Buenos Aires proposed several political and administrative reforms that, like the suppression of the cabildos, changed the structure of the judiciary. The government identified three key areas for the improvement of the administration of criminal justice: the need of a penal code (código penal), the establishment of legal procedures in criminal cases (código de procedimiento penal), and more transparency in the process of selection of criminal judges.[47] Jurists and the judiciary in general agreed that the penal and procedural codes were much needed, but this legislation would have to wait until the constitution was approved. Hence, the appeals court

---

[42] Jorge Myers, *Orden y virtud. El discurso republicano en el régimen rosista* (Quilmes, 1995), pp. 73–84.

[43] Decree of the Government (Triunvirato) creating a Comisión de Justicia, 18 April 1812, *Mayo Documental* (Buenos Aires, 1965), volume XI, p. 16713.

[44] See article 18, *Constitución de la Nación Argentina* (1853), with a preliminary study by Ruben Bortnik (Buenos Aires, 1983), pp. 38–9.

[45] 'Nota del presidente del Tribunal de Justicia al Gobernador', AGN, X.12.2.1, 6 Dec. 1821.

[46] Cámara de Justicia al ministro de gobierno, AGN, X.12.2.1, 12 March 1822.

[47] Ministro de gobierno a la Cámara de Justicia, AGN, X.12.2.1, 20 Aug. 1821.

put its efforts into suggesting more practical changes 'without taking the dangerous step of substantially altering the system of laws'.[48]

The appeals court looked forward to participating more in the process of selection of criminal judges. The tribunal accepted the government's practice of appointing them, but at the same time tried to limit the candidates. Diverse proposals tried to establish an examination process for the candidates (with a degree in law as a basic requirement) directly supervised by the appeals court and the Academia de Jurisprudencia. A list of three finalists would be sent to the executive authorities for the final appointment.[49] The government, on the other hand, wanted neither to limit its choices nor to devise a specific selection mechanism. This reluctance continued until the second half of the nineteenth century.

By focusing on administrative changes, the judicial authorities wanted to address the most important problems they faced in the decades after Independence. As Manuel Antonio de Castro (Director of the Academia de Jurisprudencia[50] and President of the Cámara de Justicia during most of the 1820s) pointed out, there were three factors that provoked inefficiency in the administration of criminal justice in Buenos Aires: lack of judges' auxiliaries or *procuradores*, ratification of witnesses and delays in the formation of criminal cases or *sumarios*.[51]

The first and second problems were related to restrictive budgets which resulted in an insufficient number of judicial personnel, as well as judicial administrative dependency on the police and executive authorities. This dependency was clear, for example, in the process of judicial ratification of witnesses. A colonial legal procedure that continued after Independence mandated that all witnesses whose written testimonies were part of the initial case (*sumario*) should be called to the courthouse in order to ratify or rectify what they said before the police. Judges summoned these witnesses weeks or even months after the crime was committed and they were not always easily found. Since criminal judges did not have enough employees, they had to request the assistance of the executive authorities to reach these people. Sometimes criminal judges had judicial employees for that task (*ordenanzas de a caballo*), but they were overwhelmed by the number of witnesses they had to find and summon. As Castro explained, the whole criminal process had to stop, pending the ratification of witnesses. Inter-

---

[48] Cámara de Justicia al gobernador, AGN, X.12.2.1, 6 Dec. 1821.

[49] See, for example, 'Projecto de Decreto sobre el modo de elegir los jueces de primera instancia en lo civil y criminal', AGN, X.15.2.8, 14 Oct. 1829.

[50] The Academia was founded in 1814 by Manuel Antonio de Castro, a lawyer and university professor at Chuquisaca during the late colonial period. Ricardo Levene, *La Academia de Jurisprudencia y la vida de su fundador Manuel Antonio de Castro* (Buenos Aires, 1941).

[51] 'Manuel Antonio de Castro al ministro de gobierno', AGN, X.13.8.6, 10 March 1825. See also 'Supremo Tribunal de Justicia eleva informe al gobierno proponiendo reformas en procedimientos de causas criminales', documento firmado por Manuel Antonio de Castro. *El Argos de Buenos Aires* no. 150, 14 May 1825 (Buenos Aires, 1931–1942), pp. 168–9.

estingly enough, he did not want to change or eliminate that legal step, but rather to obtain more resources for speeding up such a procedure.[52]

The ratification of witnesses constituted an example of the tensions originated between a legal principle and its application. Both colonial and post-colonial judicial authorities recognised that giving the witness a second opportunity to recall the circumstances of the case would bring transparency to the criminal process. However, the instrumentation of this legal step provoked resentment between the judicial and executive authorities, delayed the resolution of cases, and created a locus of arbitrary police power. If executive authorities or the police wanted to keep somebody in prison, they could get the testimony of a great many people at the beginning of the judicial process (*sumario*) and then take more in finding them later on for the ratification stage. Although the judge perhaps wanted to speed up the process, he still had to complete that legal phase to move on. With most of his few assistants working indoors on the *expedientes*, he had no choice but to demand, in endless letters to the chief of the police or other executive authorities, the completion of those summons.[53]

The judges and the appeals court were unwilling to ignore this and other legal steps and the executive authorities saw this determination as a sign of inefficiency. The various political factions in power described themselves as being pressured by the population to guarantee order and tranquility in Buenos Aires while the judicial branch of the government, they accused, was more concerned with missing signatures, double-checking procedures or the use of decorous language in the *expedientes*. Judges did not even show up in the courthouse and the executive authorities had to remind them of their duties.[54] Although these accusations were exaggerated, they illustrate how the issue of inefficiency in the administration of criminal justice was subject to different interpretations.

Due to their expectation of results and their suspicion that the judiciary was not doing enough, executive authorities from both unitarian and federalist political extractions bombarded the appeals court and judges with enquiries regarding the status of criminal cases. They wanted to know if *expedientes* were finished and criminals punished. The judicial practice of reporting pending criminal cases to the authorities was common in late colonial Buenos Aires. The alcaldes did it because they stayed only one year in office and they distributed the list when they left. During the 1810s this practice continued and executive authorities started to request such reports on a regular basis. Although tenured criminal judges replaced *alcaldes* at the beginning of the 1820s, governmental officials continued to enquire about criminal cases and demand 'harsh punishment' for crimi-

---

[52] Manuel Antonio de Castro al ministro de gobierno, AGN, X.13.8.6, 10 March 1825.

[53] See, for example, AHPBA, 5.5.74.5, (1819) and AGN, 7.1.83.9, (1829).

[54] For example, 'Ministro de gobierno al presidente del Tribunal de Justicia', AGN, X.15.2.8, 19 Oct. 1829.

nals as a way of keeping public order in post-colonial Buenos Aires.[55] These periodic reports were made mandatory during the Rivadavian years, a ruling which continued during the Rosas regime.[56]

The debates over the efficiency of the criminal justice system were also related to the third and perhaps most complex problem defined by Manuel Antonio de Castro: the formation of the *sumario*. In general terms, the judicial process was divided between *sumario* and *plenario*. The *sumario* consisted of collecting evidence and presenting the case. The subsequent evaluation of the submitted proof and final sentence was called the *plenario*.[57] During the colonial period and the first decade of *criollo* government, the *alcaldes* initiated many criminal cases, investigated them, evaluated the testimonies, and pronounced sentence in the first instance. They had legal and practical responsibility in both the *sumario* and the *plenario*. If the victim and/or accused was dissatisfied, he or she could appeal to the colonial *audiencia* (Cámara de Apelaciones or appeals court after 1812).

Population growth and social unrest in the transition from colonial to independent government made it more and more difficult for the *alcaldes* to deal with all criminal cases. The organisation of an urban police force after 1812 also included the function of assistants to the *alcaldes* in the initial stages of the *sumario*. Thus, urban police officers (*comisarios*) in each Buenos Aires neighbourhood began to handle many *sumarios* for criminal cases alongside the *alcaldes*. In contrast to the colonial period, police involvement took place not only during the initial stages of the judicial process (*auto cabeza de proceso*), but also during later stages of the *sumario* in both felonies and misdemeanors.[58]

When criminal judges replaced *alcaldes* in 1821, the new judicial magistrates became less involved in the *sumario* than their predecessors. *Jueces de paz* (justices of the peace) were appointed to deal with civil and criminal *sumarios*. That scheme worked in the countryside as the judges of the peace initiated the criminal case later sending it to the criminal judge in Buenos Aires for the *plenario*. However, the case of the city was different. Justices of the peace in Buenos Aires neighbourhoods concentrated their activities in civil disputes and most of the criminal cases were initiated and written by police *comisarios*. In fact, the role of the urban police in the formation of the *su-*

---

[55] Ministro de gobierno al Tribunal de Justicia, AGN, X.13.9.4, 19 Oct. 1826.

[56] 'Jueces, procuradores, y defensores deben pasar razón de las causas civiles y criminales al Ministerio de Gobierno', 3 Jan. 1822, Prado y Rojas (comp.), *Compilación de Leyes, Decretos...*, vol. II, p. 228. See also Ministro de gobierno al Tribunal de Justicia, AGN, X.15.10.3, 19 Dec 1831.

[57] Luis Méndez Calzada, *La función judicial en las primeras épocas de la independencia* (Buenos Aires, 1944), pp. 323–46.

[58] On the legal steps involved in the organisation of the Buenos Aires Police Department see Francisco L. Romay, 'Rivadavia y la organización de la policía en el derecho patrio', *Revista del Instituto de Historia del Derecho* (Buenos Aires, 1952), número 4, pp. 133–49; and Adolfo Enrique Rodríguez, *Cuatrocientos años de policía en Buenos Aires* (Buenos Aires, 1981).

mario was acknowledged by the government by the issuing of a decree in 1822 instructing *comisarios* on the information they had to compile. Before sending the *sumario* to the judge, the decree established that the police had to report to the executive authorities on the details of the criminal case.[59] Thus, police intervention in the *sumarios* gave the government a more direct involvement in, and control of, judicial and crime-related issues.

Criminal judges remained responsible for finishing the *sumario* and drafting the subsequent *plenario*. By the time they got the *expediente*, however, the course of the criminal process had already been laid out by the police. Judges could still collect new evidence, interrogate witnesses and the defendant and so forth, but sometimes weeks and even months passed between the crime and the moment the judge received the case from the *comisario* or justice of peace, reducing the possibilities of substantially modifying what had already been produced.

The appeals court of Buenos Aires disapproved of the practical consequences of the 1822 executive decree. It empowered the police over the judges, they stated, provoking delays in the administration of criminal justice: 'Many times *comisarios* compose long and meticulous *sumarios* instead of reporting just the crime and its circumstances, its author and the list of relevant witnesses. Thus, they frustrate the effectiveness of the judicial confession, delaying the legal process.'[60]

The appeals court and the judges were disappointed because they had to wait for the *sumario* from the police, but they were also dismayed because the government accused them of slowing down the resolution of criminal cases. The executive authorities justified police holding of the *expediente* for the time-consuming process of collecting evidence and searching for the crime's authors and witnesses. They perceived, however, that the case did not progress in the judge's hands as it went through a series of more formal judicial steps. Judicial and executive authority perspectives on these matters collided in criminal cases, like the murder of Francisco Alvarez in 1828, where the executive authorities pressed for rapid results.

The appeals court criticised governmental insistence on immediate resolution in that homicide by arguing that 'there was no slowdown in this case [...], only the type of delay that it is absolutely necessary for clarification, which is the first objective of the criminal process, public interest in general and the unique foundation of justice'.[61] Judge Bartolomé Cueto, in charge of the case, added that 'to abbreviate or to prolong a *sumario* does not depend on the judge's wish and will but on the nature of the case most

---

[59] Decree issued on 31 May 1822 by Governor Rodríguez and Minister Rivadavia. Prado y Rojas (comp.), *Recopilación de leyes, decretos...*, vol. II, p. 307.
[60] Tribunal de Justicia al ministro de gobierno, AGN, X.13.8.6, 10 May 1825.
[61] Tribunal de Justicia al ministerio de gobierno, AGN, X.14.9.3, 1 Aug. 1828.

of the time'.[62] Both the appeals court and judges emphasised that the police caused delays in the *sumario*.[63]

In response to judicial complaints of a conflicting division of powers, another decree was passed in 1830 preventing *comisarios* from writing *sumarios* for felonies.[64] Although the appeals court received and acknowledged that decree with satisfaction, it did not have practical application.[65] The two criminal judges of Buenos Aires were unable to deal with all the cases that occurred in both the city and countryside. After the 1830 decree, police *comisarios* were supposed to write only an initial statement on the case (*parte*), but they still ended up writing most of the *sumario*.

Hence, a few years later (as occurs even in present day Buenos Aires province), the exchange of accusations between executive and judicial authorities regarding efficiency in the administration of criminal justice continued to place the police *sumario* at the centre of the debate. The authorities demanded that the appeals court instruct criminal judges to 'simplify legal steps and even defence petitions in order to obtain a rapid resolution to the cases', while the tribunal indicated that the problem was 'the long interval between the moment when the crime is committed and the time when the judge finally gets the case [*sumario*] and the accused is made available to him [by the police]'.[66]

Conclusions

'Justice commissions', autonomous police practices and a dilatory administration of justice were considered non-desirable, but momentary, aspects of the emerging penal system. Those temporary aspects can be associated with the idea, developed by José Chiaramonte, of a post-colonial judicial order originally conceived as provisional after 1810, but that became permanent in the long run.[67] Intellectuals and lawmakers debated over this issue and the role of the judiciary in post-Independence Buenos Aires. Reviewing the shortcomings of the 1810 *Criollo* Revolution, Esteban Echeverría described the profile of the future ideal magistrate in 1837 as 'temporary guardian and executor of the laws. Outside the law, without

---

[62] 'Juez en lo criminal Bartolomé Cueto al Tribunal de Justicia', AGN, X.14.9.3, 31 July 1828.
[63] Another example of problems with police *sumarios* can be found in 'Juez de primera instancia en lo criminal Manuel Insiarte al Tribunal de Justicia', AGN, X.15.2.8, 9 Nov. 1829.
[64] Decree issued on 18 Dec. 1830, 'Comisarios de Policía: se revoca el decreto que los facultaba para levantar sumarios por escrito sobre delitos cometidos en sus respectivas secciones'. Prado y Rojas (comp.), *Recopilación de leyes, decretos...*, vol. III, p. 480.
[65] 'Cámara de Justicia acusa recibo de la nota del Ministerio de Gobierno revocando los decretos de 1822 y 1825 sobre sumarios', AGN, X.15.7.2, 20 Dec. 1830.
[66] Nota del ministro de gobierno a la Cámara de Justicia y respuesta de la Cámara al gobierno el 17 sept. 1833. AGN, X.16.3.3, 10 Sept. 1833,
[67] José Carlos Chiaramonte, 'El federalismo argentino en la primera mitad del siglo XIX', Marcello Carmagnani (coord.), *Federalismos latinoamericanos: Mexico/Brasil/Argentina* (Mexico, 1993), pp. 81–3.

the law, beyond the law, there are no magistrates only usurpers'.[68] Judges, however, could not prevent the increasing power of other law enforcement agents like the police. This arbitrary power eventually became a characteristic feature of the modern penal system in Argentina.

Colonial penal law remained a part of the legal architecture of Argentina at least until the second half of the nineteenth century. However, liberal principles such as due process and the defendant's rights, were also introduced immediately after 1810. Hence, the argument for continuity has to be debated in the context of everyday practices of justice administration rather than reduced to the study of criminal law.

The egalitarian discourse on the application of penal law contradicted the perceived need for effective policies of social control in early nineteenth-century Buenos Aires. These policies were carried out by adapting colonial penal practices and procedures to a post-Independence scenario while at the same time involved changing power relations in the judiciary. After 1810, the police gained more autonomy in crime-related issues.

Politicians, lawmakers and jurists recognised the significance of liberal principles as basic components of the post-independent penal system in Argentina. However, they concluded that the application of criminal justice based on this creed was not possible because of unstable political circumstances. Thus, debates regarding the ideal role of the judiciary and criminal law conceptualised the new penal system as a result but not as an instrument in the consolidation of new state forms. Meanwhile, the adaptation of colonial criminal procedures applied by empowered law enforcement agents not only functioned as transitional figure in the post-colonial judicial structure but also remained as a permanent feature of the system.

---

[68] Esteban Echeverria, *Los ideales de mayo y la tiranía (1837)* (Buenos Aires, 1944), p. 76.

CHAPTER 6

The Education of Lawyers and Judges in Argentina's *Organización Nacional* (1860–1880)

Eduardo Zimmermann

The relevance of lawyers and jurists in the nineteenth-century Latin American nation-building process is well established. Jurists were in charge of the elaboration of constitutions, codes, and legislation that would shape and regulate the political, economic and social life of the new nations. Lawyers were also active participants in the creation of the new judicial institutions that would interpret those regulations. Last but not least, as a profession, the law was the foremost channel of recruitment for the political elites that would enforce them.

The establishment of a new set of legal and judicial institutions clearly touched upon both the public and private dimensions of the new societies: debates about the suitability of different constitutional models, or the need to protect the autonomy of judicial institutions from the influence of political power, were accompanied by a process of regulation of basic social institutions associated with the private sphere, such as marriage, the family and property.[1] As has been mentioned by Víctor Uribe, lawyers were also instrumental in the emergence of an embryonic 'public sphere' in the new independent nations, both as participants in the institutions of a new political sociability — such as masonic lodges, political clubs, literary associations and salons — and as promoters of the ideological transformation that would ultimately evolve into a new politics of public opinion.[2]

---

[1] On the role of jurists on these questions in post-revolutionary France, see Donald R. Kelley and Bonnie G. Smith, 'What Was Property? Legal Dimensions of the Social Question in France (1789–1848)', *Proceedings of the American Philosophical Society*, vol. 128, no.3, (1984), p. 202:

> In the ranks of nineteenth-century intellectuals, *socialists* were a largely eccentric and excluded force, *political economists* were only beginning to find recognition and a measure of respect for their discipline, while *political theorists* were often doctrinally derivative and remote from practical social questions and consequences. It was rather the *jurists*, practicing as well as academic, who treated the problems of society, especially property, in terms that were at once closer to institutional reality and more sensitive to immediate demands and consequences.

[2] See Víctor M. Uribe, 'Colonial Lawyers, Republican Lawyers and the Administration of Justice in Spanish America', in this book. On the origins of a politics of public opinion and a bourgeois public sphere in Buenos Aires during the Organización Nacional, see Hilda Sabato, 'Citizenship, Participation and the Formation of the Public Sphere in Buenos Aires 1850s–1880s', *Past and Present*, no. 136, Aug. 1992. For an interpretation of lawyers as promoters of a new politics of public opinion during the French Old Regime, see David A. Bell, *Lawyers and Citizens. The Making of a Political Elite in Old Regime France* (Oxford, 1994).

This chapter deals with one aspect of the process of construction of Argentine judicial institutions in the nineteenth century: the issue of the relative abundance or scarcity of lawyers and the role played by universities in the education of lawyers and jurists in post-Rosas Argentina. This issue was an important component in the nineteenth-century polemics about whether education (conceived as an education in the humanities) or technical instruction were the models to follow in order to lead the country to progress and civilisation.[3]

The education of lawyers and jurists, however, also implied an 'internal' problem: an education in the law could be seen as a process of accumulation of knowledge and specialisation in certain particular areas, selected because of their perceived relevance at a given moment. This will be illustrated by the ways in which, at different moments, Constitutional Law and Civil Law occupied a place of preference in the education of the new *abogados*. Concerns about the constitutional foundation of the basic political institutions of the country coexisted with discussions about the regulation of key social institutions, such as marriage, the family and private property and its modes of transmission, and these concerns were reflected in the distribution of topics of specialisation among the new lawyers.[4]

Before entering the analysis of these topics, the next section provides an overview of the evolution of the administration of justice in independent Argentina, with particular emphasis on Federal Judicial Power after 1863, its problems and limitations, and the way in which the relative scarcity of lawyers and jurists was perceived as a fundamental cause of its shortcomings: finding men with an adequate training in the law who were willing and able to be in charge of a *juzgado* in a remote province, or legislators capable of studying and discussing in depth the draft of some complex piece of legislation, was not an easy task in nineteenth-century Argentina.[5]

---

[3] On the debates between Alberdi and Sarmiento on the role of education in nineteenth-century Argentina, see Natalio Botana, *La tradición republicana. Alberdi, Sarmiento y las ideas políticas de su tiempo* (Buenos Aires, 1984), cap. VI, pp. 263–337.

[4] Obviously, there were other areas of great importance in the process of definition of the country's basic institutions, in particular, criminal law. For a study on the links between criminal law and the definition of public order in nineteenth-century Argentina, see Mark D. Szuchman, *Order, Family and Community in Buenos Aires 1810–1860* (Stanford, 1988), chapter 2 'Disorder and Social Control'. See also Lyman L. Johnson (ed.), *The Problem of Order in Changing Societies. Essays on Crime and Policing in Argentina and Uruguay, 1750–1940* (Albuquerque, 1990); and Osvaldo Barreneche, 'Criminal Justice and State Formation in Early Nineteenth-Century Buenos Aires, Argentina', in this book. The teaching of Political Economy at the nineteenth-century law schools is another area which merits further research.

[5] These difficulties are analysed in more detail in Eduardo Zimmermann, 'El Poder Judicial, la construcción del estado, y el federalismo: Argentina, 1860–1880', in Eduardo Posada-Carbó (ed.), *In Search of a New Order: Essays on the Politics of Nineteenth-Century Latin America* (London, 1998).

Lawyers and judicial institutions in independent Argentina[6]

With the abolition of *cabildos* in 1821, the first *juzgados letrados* were set up, presided by *jueces letrados*, who enjoyed relative stability in their positions and a regular income. In 1824 judicial jurisdictions in the *campaña* were eliminated, and although *jueces de paz* remained, the administration of justice was centralised in the cities. The Rosas era, marked by a heavy concentration of political power and administrative functions through the granting of the *suma del poder público* to the dictator, represented a step back in the process of organisation and consolidation of an independent judicial power, which would be delayed until the sanction of the national Constitution of 1853, following the fall of Rosas.[7] In the field of ideas, the romantic and historicist reactions against the institutional experiments of the first generation of Independence reformers inspired by Enlightenment rationalism, were superseded by a new transformation: national liberalism as represented by Bartolomé Mitre — the political backbone of the 1860 constitutional reform, the building up of the federal judiciary, and the sanction of the first national codes of civil and commercial legislation — was mostly fuelled by a renewed dose of progressive rationalism.[8]

Since 1854 the government of the Argentine Confederation had tried with little success to establish the National Judicial Power as sanctioned by the 1853 Constitution. Articles 94 to 103 of that text followed closely article 3, second part, of the Constitution of the United States, setting up a Judicial Power composed of a Supreme Court and lesser tribunals created by Congress. In the early 1860s, under the presidency of Bartolomé Mitre, along with the reconciliation of Buenos Aires and the rest of the Confederation, the National Congress organised the federal judiciary appointing the first Supreme Court and the so-called *juzgados de sección* (federal tribunals in each capital city of the provinces).[9]

---

[6] Studies on the development of Argentine judicial institutions have focused almost exclusively — at least for the period up to the sanction of the national Constitution of 1853 — on the province of Buenos Aires. An exception to this is Víctor Tau Anzoátegui, 'La administración de justicia en las provincias argentinas (1820–1853)', *Revista de Historia del Derecho*, no. 1, 1973, pp. 205–49. See also Abelardo Levaggi, 'Establecimiento de la justicia federal en Entre Ríos (1863–1883)', *Revista de Historia del Derecho*, no. 22, (1994), pp. 177–225.

[7] Tau Anzoátegui, 'La administración de justicia', pp. 234–6. For differing interpretations on legal discourse and the administration of justice under Rosas, however, see Jorge Myers, 'Restoration of the Laws: The Discourse of the Law and the Concept of Order in Rosista Argentina 1829–1852', ms., 1995 Latin American Studies Association meeting, and his book, *Orden y virtud: el discurso republicano en el régimen rosista* (Buenos Aires, 1995); Ricardo Salvatore, 'El imperio de la ley: delito, estado y sociedad en la era Rosista', *Delito y Sociedad. Revista de Ciencias Sociales*, vol. 3, no. 4–5 (1993); Juan Carlos Garavaglia, 'Paz, orden y trabajo en la campaña: la justicia rural y los juzgados de paz en Buenos Aires, 1830–1852', *Desarrollo Económico*, vol. 37, no. 146, (1997), pp. 241–62.

[8] Cf. Víctor Tau Anzoátegui, *Las ideas jurídicas en la Argentina (siglos XIX–XX)* (Buenos Aires, 1977). See Tulio Halperín-Donghi, 'Una nación para el desierto argentino', in T. Halperín-Donghi (ed.), *Proyecto y construcción de una nación. (Argentina 1846–1880)* (Caracas, 1980) for a wider analysis of political ideas in post-Rosas Argentina.

[9] *Registro Nacional*, 1863, pp. 49–73, for the organisation of the federal tribunals (*Leyes* 48,

From then on, federal judges in the interior provinces gradually became effective representatives of the power of the national state, although they frequently had to face difficult situations arising from the continuous upheavals promoted by local *caudillos* and provincial political elites in their resistance to the national government in Buenos Aires.[10]

As has been mentioned, one of the main obstacles in this process of institutional construction was the relative scarcity of human resources available. Despite claims that the number of lawyers in the region was excessive — claims dating from the late colonial period and up to the early independent years — by mid-century, official reports, particularly from the interior provinces, made constant references to the scarcity of lawyers as a serious hindrance to the organisation of the new judicial institutions.[11] During the first half of the century, this obstacle had been solved by a system of lay justice, in which the people chose noted citizens 'de luces y conocida honradez', or 'de ilustración y probidad' to administer justice. In other cases, judicial functions were taken up by the provincial governor.[12]

With the establishment of the federal judicial system, however, the lack of professional jurists to fill the new positions became an acute problem. In addition, this issue also reflected the unbalanced distribution of human capital between Buenos Aires and the interior. According to the 1869 First National Census, of the total number of 439 lawyers in the country, more than half resided in Buenos Aires. In some of the interior provinces (San Luis, Santiago del Estero, Mendoza, La Rioja, Jujuy) the total number of lawyers was below ten.[13] It was in some of these provinces that the lack of autonomy of the judicial authorities was felt more intensely: 'hay provincias en que, por ejemplo, se mete media población a la cárcel porque se le antoja a un jefe político', claimed *El Nacional* with some exaggeration, shortly after the establishment of the *juzgados federales*. And a federal judge complained about the consequences of the absence of a prosecutor in his province: 'librar al celo de los particulares la persecución y castigo de los delitos, en países como los nuestros, acostumbrados por causas bien conocidas a dejarlo todo a la vigilancia de los funcionarios y autoridades, es consagrar su impunidad'.[14] Moreover, since there was no official register of lawyers in the country, the appointment of judges and officials in these

---

49, and 50). On the origins of the Federal Judicial Power see Clodomiro Zavalía, *Historia de la Corte Suprema de Justicia de la República Argentina* (Buenos Aires, 1920).

[10] For the role played by the *jueces federales* in several provincial uprisings against the national government, see Eduardo Zimmermann, 'El Poder Judicial'.

[11] See Víctor Uribe, 'Colonial Lawyers, Republican Lawyers', for comparative estimates of lawyers in colonial and independent Spanish America.

[12] Tau Anzoátegui, 'La administración de justicia', pp. 241–3.

[13] See Zimmermann, 'El Poder Judicial' for numbers of lawyers in the interior provinces.

[14] 'Jueces seccionales', *El Nacional*, 6 Feb. 1863; Saturnino M. Laspiur (juez federal de Córdoba), in *Memoria del Ministerio de Justicia, Culto, e Instrucción Pública*, 1869, p. 166. See Zimmermann 'El Poder Judicial' for the vicissitudes faced by the *jueces federales* in the interior provinces.

provinces required an extensive investigation by the authorities in order to verify the candidates' qualifications.[15]

The relative scarcity of lawyers was aggravated by the pressure exerted by the political process on the scant offer of jurists: lawyers were usually called to occupy the highest political positions in their respective provinces, this being another tradition dragged down from early independent life. During the whole nineteenth century observers criticised this tendency to 'entrar al Poder Judicial como medio de escalar otra posición política'.[16] The connections between the legal world and the political arena were inevitable, more so in the case of the federal judges acting as representatives of the national state in the provinces, and judges and lawyers frequently alternated between judicial and political appointments, which made a genuine process of differentiation of the two spheres very difficult.[17] Ironically, this continuous interplay between politics and the law was also instrumental in the characterisation of the 'abogados revoltosos' and their struggles for power as a factor of political instability in nineteenth-century Latin America, and the subsequent claims about the dangerous consequences arising from the abundance of lawyers in the new societies.[18]

Jurists as men of letters

As has been mentioned, despite the persistence of a discourse that stressed the dire consequences of the lack of well trained jurists in the country, an opposite line of thought had always been present in the public debate, one which saw an alleged overabundance of lawyers, and by extension of men of letters in general, as one of the most dangerous features of the new societies.

There was, therefore, a 'legalist-institutional' discourse which looked upon lawyers as the most genuine interpreters of the science of government, and thus

---

[15] See Norberto C. Dagrossa, 'Los acuerdos del Senado (1854–1877)', *Revista de Historia del Derecho*, no. 18, 1990, pp. 25–131, and no. 19, 1991, pp. 133–208, for the debates in the National Senate on the appointment of federal judges.

[16] Raimundo Wilmart, in *Revista Jurídica*, 1899, quoted by Clodomiro Zavalía, *Historia de la Corte Suprema*. p. 16. Zavalía himself was not that critical, considering that political experience for a jurist was 'como un soplo de la realidad de la vida que se lleva para sacudir un tanto a los que están envejeciendo en la fría aplicación de la ley', p. 18.

[17] In the case of the federal judges in Argentina, from the first sixty appointments to the Supreme Court and the *juzgados de sección* between 1863 and 1880 practically all of these (there was no information available for eight cases) occupied political positions at provincial or national level, before or after their assignment. Zimmermann, 'El Poder Judicial', pp. 4–5. For the political uses of the judiciary after 1880, see Eduardo Saguier, 'La magistratura como herramienta de contienda política. La justicia federal en el siglo XIX de la Argentina', *Actas del Primer Congreso de Investigación Social: Región y Sociedad en Latinoamérica* (Universidad Nacional de Tucumán, 1995), pp. 113–23. For a more general analysis, see the classic study on the evolution of administrative recruitment processes in modern Europe by Wolfram Fischer and Peter Lundgren, 'The Recruitment and Training of Administrative and Technical Personnel', in Charles Tilly (ed.), *The Formation of National States in Western Europe* (Princeton, New Jersey, 1975), pp. 456–561.

[18] See Víctor Uribe, 'Colonial Lawyers, Republican Lawyers'.

as the main actors of the state-building process; and a 'technical-practical' discourse which deplored, as a prominent and highly pernicious feature of Hispanic American political culture, the higher standing that lawyers, and men of letters in general, enjoyed over scientists, engineers, industrialists and tradesmen. These opposing camps would adopt very different positions regarding the role that higher education was to play in the political, economic and social transformation of the new nations.

For the Argentine case, perhaps the most representative critic of the alleged over-abundance of men of letters was Juan Bautista Alberdi. A lawyer himself, Alberdi was the author of the 1852 *Bases*, a book which inspired much of the 1853 Argentine Constitution. In his book, Alberdi expressed his misgivings about the consequences for the new republics of what he saw as an overvaluation of a system of higher education strongly biased towards the humanities:

> La instrucción superior en nuestras repúblicas, no fue menos estéril e inadecuada [que la instrucción primaria] a nuestras necesidades. ¿Qué han sido nuestros institutos y universidades de Sud-América, sino fábricas de charlatanismo, de ociosidad, de demagogia y de presunción titulada? ... La instrucción para ser fecunda ha de contraerse a ciencias y artes de aplicación, a cosas prácticas, a lenguas vivas, a conocimientos de utilidad material e inmediata ... El plan de instrucción debe multiplicar las escuelas de comercio y de industria, fundándolas en pueblos mercantiles. Nuestra juventud debe ser educada en la vida industrial y para ello ser instruida en las artes y ciencias auxiliares de la industria. El tipo de nuestro hombre sud-americano debe ser el hombre apto para vencer al grande y agobiante enemigo de nuestro progreso: el desierto, el atraso material, la naturaleza bruta y primitiva de nuestro continente.[19]

Alberdi's preference for the civilising effects of commerce and industry, and his critique of the glorification of political struggles and military heroism, which he saw as pervading the political culture of the first half-century of independent life and being perpetuated through the educational system, was to remain central in his system of ideas.

A quarter of a century after *Bases*, Alberdi insisted on this line of thought in two important works. The first, a biography of the US entrepreneur William Wheelwright, promoter of railway lines in various Latin American countries,[20] is an emphatic vindication of commerce and industry as the true vehicles of transformation in South America. The spirit of industry incarnated in the immigrants, and not formal education, was the key to genuine progress: 'la instrucción no educa el alma ni el carácter sino muy secundariamente. Deja, con frecuencia, al hombre en la plenitud de su barbarie primitiva ...' The living presence of men like Wheelwright, by contrast, was an example of the beneficial influence of the Anglo-Saxon presence in Latin America. Wheelwright was 'el tipo de hombre que Su-

---

[19] Juan Bautista Alberdi, *Bases y puntos de partida para la organización política de la República Argentina* (1852), in *Obras Completas* (Buenos Aires, 1888).
[20] Juan Bautista Alberdi, *La vida y los trabajos industriales de William Wheelwright en la América del Sud* (1876), in his *Obras Completas* (Buenos Aires, 1887), vol. VIII.

damérica necesita si quiere emular los progresos de la sociedad norteamericana... el héroe de la paz, que representa el progreso, porque representa el vapor, la electricidad aplicados como fuerzas al servicio del hombre'.

In *Escritos Económicos*, also written in 1876 though published posthumously, Alberdi insisted that 'el menor hacendado, el simple labrador, el humilde gaucho' contributed to the creation of wealth and to the civilising process in South America much more than 'todos nuestros literatos y poetas y retóricos y oradores más pintados y más pretensiosos'. Moreover, the predominance of 'los hombres ilustrados' led to the elevation of their interests: 'la literatura histórica, la política militante, la poesía, el teatro, la prensa periódica, el romance, la jurisprudencia, la teología, en una palabra, las ciencias morales', and this exaltation produced the rebirth of the kind of passions and 'enthusiasm' which science, industry and 'doux commerce' were supposed to mitigate:

> La ciencia apacigua, la literatura exalta. La ciencia es la luz, la razón, el pensamiento frío y la conducta reflexiva. La literatura es la ilusión, el misterio, la ficción, la pasión, la elocuencia, la armonía, la ebriedad del alma: *el entusiasmo*. ... Las consecuencias sociales de esa dirección dada a la cultura intelectual es la exaltación y el entusiasmo en los espíritus, la exageración, la vanidad y el orgullo, que se ofende de la crítica y de la contradicción en lo general de los hombres públicos que figuran en las letras, en la política, en la prensa, en las cosas de gobierno.[21]

If there was a danger that political passions and enthusiasms kindled by the men of letters led to the recurrent political instability which Alberdi feared so much, there were also serious economic consequences from the predominance of jurists and men of letters in Argentine universities. 'El único producto nacional y propio de las universidades de Sudamérica es el doctor en leyes o el abogado', claimed Alberdi, 'rarísimo es el hombre de ciencia que no sea europeo'. The inability to produce a 'technical elite' in the country was noted constantly in the press and official publications. In 1870, the newspaper *El Nacional*, in a critique of government intervention in the design of university

---

[21] Juan Bautista Alberdi, *Escritos económicos* (1876), in *Escritos póstumos* (Buenos Aires, 1895–1901), vol. I, chapter 8. The concept of 'enthusiasm' used by Alberdi is taken from Adam Smith, quoted by Alberdi, although with a different meaning: while Smith exalted science as 'the great antidote to the poison of enthusiasm and superstition', Alberdi points more specifically to enthusiasm as a symptom of *political* passions. Alberdi also misquotes Smith in stating that, according to the author of *The Wealth of Nations*, holidays and public celebrations nurtured enthusiasm. Smith, however, stated that these occasions operated as remedies against the sources of enthusiasm and superstition. See Adam Smith, *An Inquiry into the Nature and Causes of the Wealth of Nations* (1776), book V, chapter I , part III, article 'Of the Expense of the Institutions for the Instruction of People of all Ages'. For the classic analysis of political passions and the men of letters at the time of the French Revolution, see Alexis de Tocqueville, *L'Ancien régime et la révolution* (1856), part III, chapter I . For the different images of the of men of letters forged during the eighteenth century, see Roger Chartier, 'El hombre de letras', in Michelle Vovelle, et al., *El hombre de la Ilustración* (Madrid, 1995). See also Albert Hirschmann, *The Passions and the Interests* (Princeton, New Jersey, 1977) for the intellectual roots of the idea of the civilising effects of 'doux commerce'.

programmes, picked up Alberdi's arguments, stating that intervention from the ministry reinforced the traditional preference for the law, the arts, and the humanities: 'la juventud argentina tiene que abrazar forzosamente la abogacía'. This was particularly distressing at a time when it had become clear to *El Nacional* that the material progress of the country depended on government support to an education in the sciences, engineering and technology:

> El porvenir está en manos de los que construirán los ferrocarriles, allanarán los montes, abrirán caminos y nos harán puertos. El porvenir de los pueblos, en el siglo del vapor y del telégrafo, está en poder de los ingenieros, productores agricultores e industriales de artefactos y máquinas. Más que nadie necesitamos de ingenieros, agricultores, mineros y toda clase de fabricantes, para que el país progrese en el sentido que debe, es decir, favoreciendo el desarrollo de sus riquezas naturales y la creación de industrias propias a la transformación de sus productos. Mientras tanto el argentino del interior no puede dedicarse a ninguna de estas profesiones.[22]

At that time, according to the 1869 National Census, there were in Argentina 439 lawyers and 194 engineers, and similar figures could be found in Chile (435 lawyers and 191 engineers in 1866). However, the commentary to the census made clear that Alberdi was not alone in suggesting that the problem was not only the over-abundance of lawyers, but an excessive overvaluation of the university trained professions in general over other beneficial forces in society:

> El número excesivo de abogados, de médicos, de ingenieros, de filósofos, de literatos, no siempre puede ser motivo para mejora de la ciencia, ni de la sociedad, ni para la condición de número igual de individuos. Por el contrario, tal vez sea un mal ensanchar las esferas de las aspiraciones, en razón excesivamente alta con relación a las que la sociedad puede satisfacer.

Two types of negative consequences arose from this lack of proportion between the size of the 'university class' and the needs of society. On the one hand, university educated men were frequently overenthusiastic about the originality of their own thought, and quickly degenerated into mere charlatans: 'millares de fabricadores de filosofía que no se entiende a sí misma; inventores de sistemas políticos que prometen gratis perfección absoluta y vida sin dolores; descubridores de panaceas y de movimiento perpetuo'. On the other hand, there was also the threat of a serious disequilibrium between aspirations and achievements for this class, which could end in the emergence of an intellectual proletariat, 'un verdadero pauperismo ilustrado', which would feed the ever present dangers of social unrest and revolution, aided now by 'la internacional y el comunismo'.[23]

---

[22] 'La instrucción en la República. Ramos útiles que faltan', *El Nacional*, 15 January 1870. For the attempts to create a technical elite in Colombia, see Frank Safford, *The Ideal of the Practical. Colombia's Struggle to Form a Technical Elite* (Austin and London, 1976).

[23] *Primer Censo Nacional*, 1869, 'Introducción', pp. xliii–xlv. Fears about the dangers of an 'intellectual proletariat', allegedly composed mostly of lawyers, were also common in Europe. For the

Probably inspired by less alarming arguments, the rector of the University of Buenos Aires, Juan María Gutiérrez, had included in his 1860s reforms the creation of a department of sciences (ciencias exactas) and hired a number of Italian professors of mathematics, natural history and geology. The first engineers from the newly-created department graduated in 1869. Nevertheless, the disparity between the numbers of students of the law and other fields remained throughout this period: between 1874 and 1880 the University of Buenos Aires received 326 doctoral dissertations in law, 188 in medicine, and only 25 in mathematics.[24]

The education of jurists in nineteenth-century Argentine universities

Before the establishment of the Universidad de Buenos Aires in 1821, and due to the predominance of theological studies at the Universidad de Córdoba, the study of the law for the River Plate students frequently implied a trip to Chuquisaca or Santiago de Chile, and for the more affluent ones to the Real Universidad de San Carlos de Lima, or even to Spain.[25] At Buenos Aires, the department of jurisprudence was arranged around two chairs: Derecho Natural y Público de Gentes, given to Antonio Sáenz, the first rector of the University, and Derecho Civil, given to Pedro Somellera. Later on, chairs in Canon Law and Political Economy were added, although the latter was suppresed after a short period.[26]

The *rosista* age resulted in a serious degradation of the teaching of jurisprudence and of the general management of the university as well. The emergence of a young, liberal opposition to Rosas gave new impulse to the study of legal ideas: Juan Bautista Alberdi's *Fragmento preliminar al estudio del derecho* (1837),[27] and the doctoral dissertations of Juan María Gutiérrez (1834) and Manuel Quiroga de la Rosa (1838), reflected the anxious search that the new generation made in the study of law in order to find a suitable foundation for their political philosophy and a guide in their campaign against *rosismo*. In his

---

Italian case, see Andrea Camelli, 'Universities and professions', and Aldo Mazzacane, 'A Jurist for United Italy: the Training and Culture of Neapolitan Lawyers in the Nineteenth Century', in Maria Malatesta (ed.), *Society and the Professions in Italy, 1860–1914* (Cambridge, 1995), pp. 57, 109.

[24] Tulio Halperín-Donghi, *Historia de la Universidad de Buenos Aires* (Buenos Aires, 1962), pp. 73–6; Marcial R. Candioti, *Bibliografía doctoral de la Universidad de Buenos Aires y catálogo cronológico de las tesis en su primer centenario, 1821–1920* (Buenos Aires, 1920), p. 208. On the role played by Juan María Gutiérrez as rector of the University of Buenos Aires in the organisation of the engineering and sciences programmes at the University, see Jorge Myers, 'Sísifo en la cuna o Juan María Gutiérrez y la organización de la enseñanza de la ciencia en la universidad argentina', *Redes*, vol. 1, no. 1, Sept. 1994, pp. 113–31.

[25] Enrique Arana (h), 'Nuestra bibliografía jurídica retrospectiva (1810–1852)', in *II Congreso Internacional de Historia de América* (Buenos Aires, 1938), vol. V, p. 9.

[26] Candioti, *Bibliografía doctoral*, pp. 47–8

[27] Juan Bautista Alberdi, *Fragmento preliminar al estudio de derecho* (1837) (Buenos Aires, 1944).

Recuerdos de provincia, Sarmiento described the impression made by the arrival in San Juan of Quiroga de la Rosa in 1838. Recently graduated from the Universidad de Buenos Aires, the young lawyer was 'lleno de fe y entusiasmo en las nuevas ideas que agitaban el mundo literario de Francia ... : Jouffroy, Lerminier, Guizot, Cousin, en filosofía e historia; Tocqueville, Pedro Lerroux, en democracia...'. Alberdi's *Fragmento* also marked a new beginning in legal philosophy, being a typical exponent of the historicist movement inspired by the writings of Savigny and Lerminier which was gradually to replace the prevailing rationalism in the university courses, as exemplified by Bentham's influence in Somellera's course on civil law.[28]

After the fall of Rosas in 1852, new courses were opened on criminal and commercial law, and the chair in political economy was reintroduced. With the arrival of Juan María Gutiérrez as rector in 1861, there were deeper changes in the structure and content of legal studies. Gutiérrez abolished the Academia de Jurisprudencia, where candidates had to take three years of professional practice, and widened the curriculum with the introduction of new courses: Roman Law in 1863; Constitutional Law in 1868, Legal Medicine in 1871, and Procedural Law in 1873. Finally, in 1874 the old Departamento de Jurisprudencia changed its name to Facultad de Derecho y Ciencias Sociales, as it is known today.[29]

An overview of the catalogue of doctoral dissertations presented at the Buenos Aires Law School between the 1820s and the 1880s reveals the distribution of the preferences for particular subjects among the students. Between 1821 and 1851, over a total of 179 dissertations, 112 were on topics of civil law; 20 on criminal law; 11 on 'derecho natural y de gentes'; 10 on legal philosophy and jurisprudence; 10 on canon law; 8 on political economy; and 8 on various other subjects. The complete absence of dissertations on constitutional law during this period is explained by the fact that there was no chair of constitutional law in Buenos Aires until 1868. Between 1852 and 1873, of over a total of 243 dissertations, 108 were on topics of civil law, 38 on political economy (the chair having been reintroduced in 1852), 36 on constitutional and administrative law, 33 on criminal law, 14 on commercial law, seven on international law, one on canon law and six on various subjects. The growing interest in constitutional law is explained by the creation of the chair in 1868; also, the national Constitution had been sanctioned in 1853 and reformed in 1860, and there was intense public debate on the reform of the province of Buenos Aires Constitution in 1870–1873. Finally, between 1874 and 1880, over a total of 326 dissertations, 129 were on topics of civil law, 65 on constitutional law, 40 on commercial law, 40 on criminal law, 37 on political economy and 15 on various subjects.

A similar distribution of preferences can be found among the Buenos Aires graduates appointed as federal judges during this period. Of the first 60 ap-

---

[28] Domingo Faustino Sarmiento, *Recuerdos de provincia* (1850) (Buenos Aires, 1944), p. 248; Candioti, *Bibliografía doctoral*, p. 52.
[29] Halperín-Donghi, *Historia de la Universidad de Buenos Aires*, pp. 71–6; Candioti, *Bibliografía Doctoral*, pp. 114–15, 209.

pointments as federal judges between 1863 and 1880, 29 had graduated in Córdoba, 18 in Buenos Aires, five in Chuquisaca, and two in Montevideo (no information was available on the remaining six).[30] Of those 18 judges who had graduated in Buenos Aires, six had written their dissertations on civil law topics, three on criminal law, two on constitutional law and two on political economy. The rest were on various subjects. Clearly, not only future federal judges received their instruction at Buenos Aires. A large fraction of the late nineteenth-century Argentine political elite was educated in constitutional matters or the civil law during those years. For example, in 1869 the list of graduates receiving their degree as Doctores en Jurisprudencia included such names as Carlos Pellegrini, Leandro N. Alem, Pedro Goyena, Aristóbulo del Valle, José Terry, Norberto Quirno Costa, and José María Rosa.[31]

Constitutional law: the science of government and the US model

'All our judges and lawyers must be well versed in our federal judicial system, which they cannot apprehend from the mere text of our Constitution without a previous and detailed study of the foremost authors of North American federal law.' Thus did *El Nacional* justify in 1863 the government's decision to make available in libraries and courts of justice all over the country the most important works on the constitutional history and theory of the United States. 'Tienen que consultar a cada paso a Story...', concluded the article.[32] During the following years an impressive government effort made sure that not only Story, but many other representative names, such as *The Federalist*, Curtis, Lieber, Kent and Pomeroy, were translated into Spanish and widely distributed.[33]

Public debate on the role of the US model in Argentine constitutional practice had been intense since the first constitutional experiments in the post-independence River Plate, and had reached a peak of virulence during the mid-century polemics between Juan Bautista Alberdi and Domingo Faustino Sarmiento.[34] It took a new impulse with the establishment of the first chairs in

---

[30] Zimmermann, 'El Poder Judicial', p. 6.

[31] See Juan Silva de la Riestra, 'La pléyade de los doctores en jurisprudencia de 1869', *Académicos de Derecho y Hombres de Gobierno* (Buenos Aires, 1969), pp. 309–43.

[32] 'De la justicia federal', *El Nacional*, 5 January 1863.

[33] See *Registro Nacional*, vol. 5, 1863–1869, for a September 1863 law authorising the national executive to buy five hundred copies of José M. Cantilo's translation of Joseph Story, 'Esposición de la Constitución de los Estados Unidos, para distribuírla en los establecimientos de educación de la República'. See *Memoria del Ministerio de Justicia, Culto e Instrucción Pública*, 1865, p. 30, for a list of 'libros que se han traído de Norte América para la Biblioteca de la Exma. Corte Suprema de Justicia', including Curtis, Webster and Story, among others. Again, in *Memoria del Ministerio de Justicia, Culto e Instrucción Pública*, 1880, pp. 24–5, an inventory of the library of the Corrientes federal judge includes, among others, 'un tomo del Federalista, un tomo Derecho Constitucional (por Tiffany), un tomo Derecho Constitucional (por Story)'.

[34] For the Alberdi-Sarmiento polemics, see Botana, *La tradición republicana*. For the influence of the United States constitutional experience on Argentine practice see two articles by Ricardo Zorraquín Becú, 'La recepción de los derechos extranjeros en la Argentina durante

constitutional law, at the University of Córdoba in 1858, and at the University of Buenos Aires, in 1868, coinciding with the greater diffusion of the US model.[35] At the University of Buenos Aires, the Colombian Florentino González held the chair between 1868 and 1874. His *Lecciones de derecho constitucional*, a summary of his course published in 1869 and 1871, were a clear exposition of the interpretation of the US Constitution as a foundational document in political philosophy and constitutional practice which had to be closely followed. Political science and constitutional theory were for González an empirical science, 'una ciencia de observación', and from the study of the existing forms of government, it was clear that republican government had been most successfully established in the United States. South American constitutional practice, therefore, must be based on the detailed study of that model:

> Una teoría comprobada con los hechos satisfactorios que la práctica de ella ha producido, tiene una fuerza de convicción irresistible. La de la Constitución americana la ha tenido para mí; y creo que si los hispanoamericanos se penetran de la verdad de ella no andarán por más tiempo a ciegas en busca de la república que desean, y que no han podido realizar con combinaciones visionarias y caprichosas, como son en general las de sus constituciones políticas. La república existe, y está comprobada en los Estados Unidos por ochenta años de experiencia; no hay para qué ir a buscarla en la imaginación de los visionarios. Estudiémosla en el original.[36]

---

el siglo XIX', *Revista de Historia del Derecho*, no. 4 (1976), pp. 325–59, and 'Las fuentes de la constitución de 1853', *Revista de Historia del Derecho*, no. 16 (1988), pp. 209–47; and Abelardo Levaggi, 'Espíritu del constitucionalismo argentino de la primera mitad del siglo XIX', *Revista de Historia del Derecho*, no. 9 (1981), pp. 239–301. See also Jonathan Miller, 'The Constitutional Authority of a Foreign Talisman: A Study of US Practice as Authority in 19th Century Argentine Constitutionalism', ms.

[35] On the influence of the US Constitution on the teaching of constitutional theory and history in Argentine universities see José Carlos Chiaramonte and Pablo Buchbinder, 'Provincias, caudillos, nación y la historiografía constitucionalista argentina, 1853–1930', *Documento para discusión interna*, Instituto de Historia Argentina y Americana 'Dr Emilio Ravignani', (Buenos Aires, 1991); Emilio Ravignani, *Historia constitucional argentina* (Buenos Aires, 1930), chapter II; Héctor P. Lanfranco, 'La Cátedra de Historia y de Derecho Constitucional en la Facultad de Derecho de Buenos Aires y sus primeros maestros', *Revista del Instituto de Historia del Derecho*, no. 63 (1957), pp. 63–81; Carlos R. Melo, 'Algunos antecedentes sobre la enseñanza del derecho constitucional en las universidades argentinas', *Investigaciones y ensayos*, no. 6–7 (1969); Roberto Etchepareborda, 'Historiografía del federalismo', *Investigaciones y ensayos*, no. 14 (1973).

[36] Florentino González, *Lecciones de derecho constitucional* (1869; 2nd. ed., París, 1871), p. 430. In the second edition, González acknowledges that the book was welcomed in all Spanish American countries, 'por ser la primera obra escrita en español en que se desenvuelve la teoría del gobierno republicano tal como ha sido reducido a la práctica en los Estados Unidos'. During the 1870s González's *Lecciones*, were used as an important source of Argentine constitutional theory and doctrine at the Buenos Aires Law School. See, for instance, references in the general introductory treatise by Juan José Montes de Oca, *Introducción general al estudio del derecho* (Buenos Aires, 1877), pp. 327–9. For a biographical study of Florentino González, spanning his political activities in Colombia and his exile in Chile in the early 1860s, see J.M. Torres Caicedo, 'El Doctor Don Florentino González', *La Revista de Buenos Aires*, vol. XVI, 1868, pp. 299–320

Along the same lines, José Luis Cantilo introduced his 1868 translation of *The Federalist Papers*:

El deseo de que se familiaricen en el país, especialmente entre la juventud estudiosa, aquellos libros en que pueda estudiarse con fruto la sabia organización política de la Gran República, que ha servido de modelo a la nuestra, nos ha decidido a emprender esta nueva traducción. ... Es un libro indispensable, como lo están mostrando las referencias que a él se hacen en los debates del parlamento, en las discusiones de la prensa y aún en las disertaciones universitarias sobre materias regidas por nuestra constitución, modelada en la de los Estados Unidos.[37]

Cantilo's reference to the 'disertaciones universitarias', was well justified. Several dissertations were written under the guidance of Florentino González on issues of constitutional theory and practice arising from the United States' experience and its relevance to the Argentine situation: Aristóbulo del Valle, 'Intervención del gobierno federal en el territorio de los estados'; Carlos Pellegrini, 'Estudio sobre derecho electoral'; Roque Suárez, 'Sistema federal'; Juan Esteban Martínez, 'Gobierno federal'; Antonio Obligado, 'La libertad de cultos'; Manuel Porcel de Peralta, 'El sufragio'; José M. Cantilo, 'Las provincias no pueden legislar en materia de competencia del Congreso Federal', among others.[38]

González's successor in the Chair of Constitutional Law between 1874 and 1884 was José Manuel Estrada. Estrada strongly modified the outlook of the course, elaborating a new interpretation of the historical background of the United States and the Argentine constitutions, and of the origins of Argentine federalism. In the latter case, far from being the result of a compact between provinces understood as sovereign entities, the Argentine nation was seen as a legacy of the administrative design of the Spanish colonial world, thus preceding the existence of the provinces, an interpretation that weakened the case for the suitability of the United States model of a federal system for Argentina, and that was to prevail in the teaching of constitutional law throughout the years that followed, carried on by Estrada's successors, Lucio V. López and Aristóbulo del Valle.[39]

Civil Law and 'the foundations of a well ordered society'

Along with all the interest aroused in academic circles by constitutional debate, from the 1860s onwards there was a growing feeling that the basic institutions of civil law were also in need of urgent redefinition in order to underpin the organisation of the country after the dark age of *rosismo*. In 1876, in his *Escritos*

---

and 416–32. See also Lanfranco, 'La Cátedra de Historia y de Derecho Constitucional'.

[37] *El Federalista. Artículos sobre la Constitución de los Estados Unidos escritos en 1788 por Mr Hamilton, Mr Madison y Mr Jay, y corregidos por los mismos autores, con un apéndice que contiene los Artículos de Confederación y la Constitución de los E.U. Traducción hecha del texto inglés por J.M. Cantilo* (Buenos Aires, 1868), pp. i–iii.

[38] See Candioti, *Bibliografía doctoral*, p. 141.

[39] Chiaramonte and Buchbinder, 'Provincias, caudillos, nación', pp. 6–10.

económicos, Alberdi summarised this feeling: 'Property and family are the foundations of a well ordered society. Both belong to the realm of private life, which is the true ground of social and public life.'[40] Although interest in constitutional and political matters did not diminish, curiosity about the appropriateness of the country's social and economic institutions regulated by private law became more noticeable with the sanction of the Argentine Civil Code in 1869. These concerns, however, had been present among the students at the University of Buenos Aires Law School for many years.

In 1848, when the threat of social revolution in Europe had its echoes in Argentine intellectual circles, Miguel Navarro Viola, a young graduate at the University of Buenos Aires defended his thesis titled 'La familia y la propiedad es la base de la sociedad'. Concerns about how best to defend the idea of private property, typical of that particular historical conjuncture, were present in this work as in many others written at the time: Emilio Torres, 'Fundamentos del derecho de propiedad' (1859), and Carlos Keen, 'El derecho de propiedad es inherente a la naturaleza humana y conforme a la utilidad social' (1863), being two of the most representative. The main purpose of these works was to establish the centrality of the family and private property to the development of civilised society, and to defend the idea that the grounds for these two institutions were to be found in natural law. With the transcendental nature of family and property thus established, there usually followed an attempt to defend the 'absolute' character of private property, a feature also present in the debates over property among French jurists of the time (always an influential source of doctrine for Argentine jurists).[41]

After the sanction of the Civil Code, the law of inheritance established by the new regulations, the topic of the succession to property in general, and the institution of civil matrimony became habitual themes for doctoral dissertations. One of the points that critics of the new Civil Code attacked more vehemently was the alleged antidemocratic and monarchical spirit that pervaded its pages, due to the influence that the Napoleonic Code and Brazilian doctrine and codification had on the Argentine drafter, Dalmacio Vélez Sarsfield. In 1868 Juan Bautista Alberdi based his critique of Vélez's project on the incompatibility between Brazilian imperial institutions and the needs of the new Argentine republican order:

> Las leyes de una monarquía no pueden convenir a una república en todo lo que tenga relación con la potestad paterna..., con el sistema hereditario, *con la*

---

[40] Alberdi, *Escritos económicos*, p. 313. For another contemporary definition of civil law as concerned mainly with the 'organización de la familia y la propiedad', see Montes de Oca, *Introducción general al estudio del derecho*, p. 410.

[41] See, for instance, 'Disertación pronunciada y sostenida por Don Emilio Torres' (1859), Colección Candioti, Biblioteca Nacional, Buenos Aires. For the debates around private property in nineteenth-century France, see Kelley and Smith, 'What Was Property?'; and Donald R. Kelley, *Historians and the Law in Postrevolutionary France* (Princeton, New Jersey, 1984), chapter 11, 'The Question of Property', pp. 127–38.

constitución de la familia democrática y republicana. La madre de familia bra-
silera, el hogar doméstico basado en el servicio servil, el súbdito de un imperio,
el hidalgo aristocrático y privilegiado por la legislación monarquista del Brasil,
¿serían los modelos de que deben ser copias las madres argentinas, las familias
argentinas, los ciudadanos de la democracia argentina?

Along the same lines, in 1869 Vicente Fidel López rejected what he saw as
Vélez's attempt to follow 'el sistema de los códigos imperiales ... y esas falsas
imitaciones de la centralización francesa, que aún bajo la forma de código civil
son de una aplicación insensata a países definitivamente democráticos y federales como los del Río de la Plata'. In particular, both critics emphasised that the
regulation of property and its modes of transmission, the law of succession, and
the institution of matrimony as established in the Civil Code were 'en completa
contradicción con el espíritu social y democrático que ha de regirnos'. Vicente
Fidel López claimed that the Argentine law of succession had to introduce a
higher degree of freedom of testation, following the example of US legislation.[42]
On the other hand, in his 1880 thesis, 'Herencias forzosas', Rómulo Etcheverry
dedicated more than three hundred pages (usually, dissertations at the Buenos
Aires Law School did not exceed fifty pages) to an exhaustive analysis of the
philosophical, constitutional, historical and legal aspects of the *'legítima heredi-
taria'* (the reserved portion of the estate of which none of the legal heirs could
be deprived). Although based on Alexis de Tocqueville´s views on the enor-
mous influence which the laws of inheritance had on 'the social state of peoples',[43] Etcheverry was not so much concerned with the issue of primogeniture
as the French writer had been, but rather aimed at the defence of the *legítima*
established by the Civil Code against those who — defending freedom of testation — attacked it as a limitation on the absolute nature of private property,
guaranteed by the national Constitution. By the end of the nineteenth century,
claimed Etcheverry, Spencerian evolutionism had already made clear that society would find a middle ground between communal property and absolute private property: 'la propiedad como toda institución manifiesta en su desarrollo
tres faces: la tesis (homogeneidad), la antítesis (la heterogeneidad), para termi-

---

[42] Juan Bautista Alberdi, 'El proyecto de Código Civil para la República Argentina' (1868), in *Obras
Completas*, vol. VII, pp. 80–135; Vicente Fidel López, 'Crítica Jurídica', *Revista de Buenos Aires*,
vol. XX, 1869, pp. 106–39. In July 1868 the newspaper *La Tribuna* attacked Alberdi for his attempt
to pound together civil legislation and the spirit of Argentine political institutions: 'los derechos
civiles no tienen nada que ver con los derechos *políticos* a que la forma de gobierno se refiere'.
[43] In *Democracy in America*, Tocqueville had said of the laws of inheritance: 'They are, it is true,
civil laws, but they should head the list of all political institutions... By their means man is armed
with almost supernatural power over the future of his fellows. When the lawgiver has once fixed
the law of inheritance, he can rest for centuries; once the impulse has been given to his handiwork,
he can take his hand away; the mechanism works by its own power and apparently spontaneously
aims at the goal indicated beforehand.' Alexis de Tocqueville, *Democracy in America*, vol. I (1835),
edited by J.P. Mayer and Max Lerner (New York, 1966), p. 60.

nar en la síntesis (el equilibrio) que es la ley constante e indestructible de toda evolución como lo demuestra Spencer...'[44]

As has been mentioned, in addition to inheritance and the transmission of property, there were other controversial issues included in the Code that were to provoke wide debate at the Buenos Aires Law School. In particular, the Code's concept of marriage and the patriarchal system of family relations established by it were to attract the harshest criticisms. On the one hand, Vélez Sarsfield had reaffirmed in the Civil Code the religious nature of matrimony, stipulating as a requirement for its celebration compliance with the rites and solemnities of the Catholic Church, leaving separation without dissolution of the matrimonial bonds as the only possible end to an irreconcilable marriage, and thus rejecting altogether the notion of civil matrimony advanced by the Napoleonic Civil Code. Vélez stated in a note to Article 167 that 'sólo a los que no profesan religión alguna puede satisfacer el matrimonio civil'. On the other hand, the Code also reaffirmed a strong conception of patriarchal authority (*patria potestad)* within the family. Women could not conduct property transactions, engage in trade, or even sign legal documents, without their husband's consent. A married woman could not share with her husband parental authority over her children.[45]

Vélez's refusal to secularise marriage, and his strong conception of *patria potestad* were rejected by many as incompatible with the new Argentine republican liberal order, as can be seen in the above mentioned criticisms of the Code made by Alberdi and Vicente Fidel López. Many doctoral dissertations at the Buenos Aires Law School also dealt with this issue, most of them defending the concept of civil matrimony, and attacking Vélez for having left 'en manos del clero el contrato más noble, el matrimonio, despojando al Estado de su derecho más sagrado, organizar las familias que son su verdadero plantel ...'[46] Along the same lines, *El Nacional* defended civil matrimony ('el progreso del siglo lo reclama'), although recognising the complexities that secularisation implied: 'la autoridad romana no

---

[44] Rómulo Etcheverry, 'Herencias forzosas' (1880), Colección Candioti, Biblioteca Nacional, Buenos Aires.
[45] *Código Civil de la República Argentina*, libro I, sección II, 'Del matrimonio'. See Donna J. Guy, 'Lower-class families, women, and the law in nineteenth-century Argentina', *Journal of Family History*, Fall, 1985, pp. 318–31, for other socioeconomic implications of *patria potestad*. In his book on *Order, Family, and Community in Buenos Aires 1810–1860*. Szuchman traces the evolution of family and polity in the first half of the nineteenth century through the concept of political patriarchy, as exemplified by Argentine *caudillos*: 'The Argentine political context — in the absence of constitutional norms and of formal and representative institutions for smooth administration — required that a time-honoured and widely recognised principle of authority be used in lieu of an institutional apparatus. Here lies the component of political authority that patriarchy provided...' (p. 231). After the sanction of the Civil Code, on the other hand, critics of Vélez tended to blame the excessive influence of imperial precedents on the legislator, rather than the country's history and custom, as the main culprit for the persistence of a patriarchal tradition.
[46] See, for instance, Leopoldo Basavilbaso, 'Del matrimonio' (1867), and Adolfo Saldías, 'Del matrimonio' (1873), in the Colección Candioti, Biblioteca Nacional, Buenos Aires.

puede ser despreciada ni tampoco es prudente hacer prescindencia de ella'.[47] Perhaps the most poignant criticism of the Code was made a decade after it became law by a young lawyer, later an influential name in Argentine politics, José Nicolás Matienzo. Reviewing a critical edition of the Civil Code published in 1881 by another jurist, Lisandro Segovia, Matienzo lamented that the author had not been critical enough of what he considered the Code's most serious shortcomings.[48] He concentrated mainly on three points: first of all, Vélez had an insufficient knowledge of the new science of political economy, and relying excessively on Romanic sources had thus produced an archaic system of regulation of private property and its modes of transmission: '¿Cómo pueden saber más sobre la naturaleza y papel social de la compra-venta Papiniano y Paulo que Adam Smith y Bastiat?'[49] Second, the patriarchal nature of family relations as established by the Code was openly against the dignity of women, and against 'the spirit of justice and liberty which animates modern science':

> Deprimir a la madre, subordinando su voluntad, su juicio y su instinto materno a la voluntad caprichosa del marido, es suprimir una personalidad que la naturaleza ha destinado a fines nobilísimos y trascendentes ... El codificador ha ido a golpear la puerta de la vieja legislación romana, desdeñosa del derecho de la mujer, y de las legislaciones anti-científicas, paganas aunque modernas, que han copiado servilmente la romana.

Finally, Matienzo also condemned Vélez's decision to maintain the rites and solemnities of the Catholic Church as a requirement for the celebration of matrimony, thus hurting protestants and the non-religious alike, on two counts. This discrimination went against the principles of equality before the law and freedom of religion, guaranteed by the national constitution and it also jeopardised official immigration policy aimed at the attraction of Anglo-Saxons: 'esas razas son protestantes en general, injuriar su conciencia es rechazarlas'.[50]

In addition to technical discussions among experts about the origins and the right interpretation of the new regulations, it was clear that there was also a series of complex political implications involved in the debates about codification. National codification had frequently been seen, both by promoters and opponents, as an important political tool, instrumental in the consolidation of a unified nation, and this was the case not only in the new Latin American nations, but in the European processes of national unification as well. In early nine-

---

[47] 'Matrimonios mixtos', *El Nacional,* 26 de noviembre de 1869.
[48] José Nicolás Matienzo, 'Un comentario del Código Civil argentino', *Nueva Revista de Buenos Aires,* vol. I, 1881, pp. 406–24. The book reviewed is Lisandro Segovia, *El Código Civil de la República Argentina, con su esplicación y crítica bajo la forma de notas* (Buenos Aires, 1881).
[49] Matienzo, 'Un comentario del Código Civil Argentino', p. 421.
[50] Matienzo, 'Un comentario del Código Civil Argentino', pp. 416–8. Arguments in favour of the secularisation of matrimony increased until the sanction of a *Ley de Matrimonio Civil* in 1888, which modified the text of the Civil Code. Legal restrictions on women, on the other hand, remained for many years. It was only in 1985, that divorce and women´s right to share in exercising *patria potestad* became legal.

teenth-century Germany, the 'battle over codification', the *Kodifikationsstreit*, provoked by the polemics between Thibaut and Savigny, involved not only a clash between different interpretations of the nature and origins of the law, and the emergence of the historical school of law which came to dominate German legal thought, but was also inextricably linked to the fate of nationalism. Legal uniformity was a powerful unifying force, and the questions concerning legal codification involved serious issues of sovereignty between the states of the German Confederation and the forces of national unification. Again, the adoption in Italy of the 1804 Napoleonic Civil Code also originated a constant interplay between the new regulations and local custom and practice in the different regions, before and after Unification.[51] For the Argentine case, the political implications of codification were summed up by Alberdi, who, just as Vicente Fidel López, was a political opponent of presidents Mitre and Sarmiento, promoters of the Civil Code:

> Los códigos no se hacen en un país por que los jurisconsultos los reclaman o los quieren. Los traen únicamente los acontecimientos políticos. Ellos son un instrumento de poder o de revolución, y no se consulta a la ciencia sobre su oportunidad.[52]

Ultimately, the sanction of the Argentine Civil Code was also under attack because it was seen by many as an important step in the process of consolidation of the *mitrista* regime, and as another sign of the transition towards centralisation at the national level. This view, nurtured in part by the conflictive relations between the Buenos Aires political elite and the Argentine provinces, affected the public debate on the merits of the project.[53] These political implications of codification were also present in the process of discussion of the Code in the universities. Doctoral dissertations dealt with issues that touched upon both constitutional and civil law, such as the constitutional power of the National Congress to sanction a National Civil Code, which left the provinces in a paradoxical situation: they retained the power to sanction their own constitutions but were

---

[51] Michael John, *Politics and the Law in Late Nineteenth-Century Germany. The Origins of the Civil Code* (Oxford, 1989), pp. 6–7, 18–20; John A. Davis, *Conflict and Control. Law and Order in Nineteenth-Century Italy* (London, 1988), pp. 122–5.

[52] Alberdi, 'El proyecto de Código Civil', p. 127. Alberdi was following the French jurist Eugène Lerminier, one of the authors through whom the thought of Savigny and the German Historical School of Law was known in Latin America. On Lerminier and French juridical thought, see Kelley, *Historians and the Law*; and Bonnie G. Smith, 'The Rise and Fall of Eugène Lerminier', *French Historical Studies*, vol. XII, no. 3, Spring 1982; on his influence in Argentina see Tau Anzoátegui, *Las ideas jurídicas en la Argentina*, pp. 53, 96.

[53] On the conflictive origins of the Civil Code, see Jorge Cabral Texo, *Historia del Código Civil Argentino* (Buenos Aires, 1920); Abel Cháneton, *Historia de Vélez Sarsfield* (Buenos Aires, 1937), 2 vols; Víctor Tau Anzoátegui, *La codificación en la Argentina (1810–1870)* (Buenos Aires, 1977); Abelardo Levaggi, 'Alberdi-Vélez Sarsfield: Una polémica trascendental sobre la codificación civil argentina', in Bravo Lira et al., *Fuentes ideológicas y normativas de la codificación latinoamericana* (Buenos Aires, 1992); and Eduardo Zimmermann, 'Ley y política: el debate en torno a la sanción del Código Civil argentino, 1868–1871', *XIV Jornadas de Historia del Derecho Argentino* (Buenos Aires, 1992).

unable to sanction particular codes. The debate on codification, therefore, was accompanied by questions about the suitability of such constitutional arrangement, which some of the students found 'contraria al espíritu de la Unión Federal y nociva al desenvolvimiento del progreso nacional'.[54] This interpretation was supported by Florentino González — professor of constitutional law and, as we have seen, a strong defender of the US juridical system — who attacked codification in general, as a pernicious legacy of Romanic and Continental juridical thought. In this he was challenged by José María Moreno, Professor of Civil Law, who defended codification and became a vindicator of the Civil Code at the Buenos Aires Law School.[55]

In fact, Moreno had to face more than the opposition of Florentino González in his campaign to make the Civil Code an object of study. Already in 1869, before the sanction of the Code, *El Nacional* claimed that the project had to be discussed in the university classrooms, and particularly in doctoral dissertations, which thus far were usually dedicated to 'materias tratadas y discutidas hasta el fastidio'. The project for the national civil code, on the other hand, was ready to serve doctoral candidates as 'una mina inagotable de riqueza para la imaginación y el talento'. The paper advised the rector, therefore, that at least some of the sections of the code should be made compulsory material for dissertations. Two years later, however, and despite the fact that the Code had become law, *La Tribuna* complained bitterly about the reduced number of copies available. In some of the provinces, stated the paper, there were only two or three copies in existence; many *jueces de paz* could not even begin to study the new regulations because they had not been able to get a copy, and even in the city of Buenos Aires, 'los estudiantes de la universidad, sobre todo, se encuentran en grandes apuros para poder cumplir el programa del aula del Derecho Civil, por que la mayor parte de ellos no tienen el código'.[56]

Despite all these practical difficulties, and with no need of the official requirement *El Nacional* had demanded, José María Moreno had been urging his students to study and discuss the project, even before it became law. In 1872, following Moreno's advice, the Civil Law course was extended to cover four years, one for each book of the Code. Moreno was so successful in his endeavor that, according to early legal historians, by the time the Code was enacted, 'a whole generation of lawyers had become acquainted with the system of the new Civil Code'.[57]

---

[54] See for instance, the 1872 dissertations by Antonio Lodola and José María Cantilo, 'Las provincias no pueden legislar en materia de competencia del Congreso Federal', in the Colección Candioti, Biblioteca Nacional, Buenos Aires.
[55] For the polemics between González and Moreno, see Tau Anzoátegui, *La codificación en la Argentina*, pp. 391–96.
[56] 'Código Civil', *El Nacional*, 2 July 1869; '¿Rige o no rige este código?', *La Tribuna*, 8 Dec. 1871.
[57] See Cabral Texo, *Historia del Código Civil*; Alberto David Leiva, 'El Código Civil como objeto didáctico en la Argentina de fines del siglo XIX', *Revista de Historia del Derecho*, no. 16, 1988.

Conclusions

There is no doubt that the need to find constitutional models designed to organise and establish limits to political power, and the regulation of basic social institutions through private law, were genuine concerns in the Argentine nation-building process in which lawyers and jurists were deeply involved. The process of adaptation of those institutions of public and private law to nineteenth-century Argentina reality proved to be complex and conflictive, and universities and law schools were deeply involved in it.

First of all, as we have seen, there were differing perceptions of the issue of the relative scarcity of lawyers and jurists in the origins of Argentine judicial institutions: there were those who argued that government should increase its efforts to improve the quality and quantity of law professionals in order to satisfy the demands imposed by the process of institutional reorganisation which followed the fall of *rosismo*. On the other hand, many others continued to identify lawyers and jurists as merely a category of the dangerous 'man of letters', too inclined towards abstract thought, detached from the real needs of society and always closer to the agitations of political life than to the practical and technical types of knowledge which the material transformation of the country demanded. Nevertheless, fear of an eventual overabundance of these men of letters and the ensuing emergence of an 'intellectual proletariat' did not prevent the process of institutionalisation of legal studies. Moreover, in a social order where law was originated not by the accumulation of juridical precedents and decisions as in a common law system, but mostly by the elaboration and adaptation of doctrine, universities and law schools found themselves at the centre of the process of creation of basic norms and regulations. Thus, debates over constitutional and civil law issues reflected not merely the intensity of academic enquiries, but the awareness among the enlightened elites of the centrality of these polemics to the institutional reorganisation of the country.

In a sense, this centrality explains why the limits between legal and judicial matters and the world of politics were often blurred, as exemplified in the debates on the suitability of US constitutional theory to the Argentine situation, on the organisation of the federal judicial system, on the influence of different civil law traditions on Argentine legislation, and on codification. Far from decreasing — as expected in a process of functional differentiation and rationalisation of authority, and despite the growth of a 'scientific' bent in legal studies after the turn of the century — the connection between law and politics, and the role played by lawyers and jurists as mediators in that relationship, were to remain a central feature of Argentine public life.